KU-535-749

THE
PEGGY & ISABELLA

The story of an
eighteenth century
Orkney sloop

Ian Hustwick

THE
ALTMACHAR
PRESS

First published in 1996 by
The Altmachar Press,
12, Baillieswells Terrace,
Bieldside,
Aberdeen.
AB15 9AR.

© Text, Ian Hustwick, 1996.

387.224
1094326

Edited by Pamela Beasant.

Cover design and page layout by Iain Ashman.

© Illustrations, Iain Ashman, 1996.

No part of this publication may be reproduced,
stored in a retrieval system, or transmitted in any
form or by any means, electronic, mechanical,
photocopying, recording or otherwise, without
the prior permission of the publisher.

Typeset in 12/14.5 Times

Printed by The Kirkwall Press,
Hell's Half Acre, Hatston,
Kirkwall, Orkney.
KW15 1DW.

ISBN 0 9529211 0 3

Cover map by an unknown French cartographer, 1757.
(By permission of The Orkney Library Archivist, ref D1.)
Full title of map:
Carte Réduite, des Isles Britanniques, Quatrieme Feuille,
Partie Septentrionale de l'Écosse Contenant
la Suite des Costes Orientales et Occidentales
Depuis Cromarty Jusqu'à Loch ou Lac Torridon
Avec les Isles d'Orkney et de Hetland.

ABOUT THE AUTHOR

Ian Hustwick, who lives in Aberdeen, comes from a
family that was engaged in shipbuilding and shipowning
in the Moray Firth for a considerable period in the18th
and 19th centuries.
He is the author of *The Moray Firth: Ships and Trade*
(Scottish Cultural Press, 1994).

ACKNOWLEDGEMENTS

I would wish to express my appreciation
for the help and advice given by
the Archivist of Orkney Public Library,
Mrs Alison Fraser, and the Assistant Archivist,
Mr Philip Astley, and to Frances Wilkins for
pointing out the wealth of information that
these archives contain. I would also wish to
thank Mrs Sue Mowat for her
advice on maritime records of the18th century.

This book is dedicated
to my wife, Patricia.

CONTENTS

CHAPTERS

Figures

Tables

Appendices

FOREWORD
BY DAVID M FERGUSON

The author has traced the career of the Kirkwall registered sloop, *Peggy and Isabella*, from her construction in 1777, to an unknown end in the early 19th century. Using 18th century shipping and estate records held in the Orkney Archives, Ian Hustwick has described her owners, construction, crews, voyages and cargoes carried. It is difficult to imagine that the creeks and smaller harbours of Orkney, now all but deserted, were once thronged with such small vessels trading directly with the rest of Great Britain and Northern Europe.

The text contains a wealth of information with splendidly arcane terms, such as "spoutage", "average" and "Master under God", described in voluminous explanatory notes.

Meticulous research by the author has produced a most invaluable book on Orkney's maritime history.

Quoybow,
Stromness
July, 1996.

Chapter one

To
Buy or Build
a Ship

In the 1770's, the Orkney Islands were experiencing considerable prosperity because of the demand for kelp from the industrial centres of the north of England and Scotland. One report in the *Old Statistical Account* of 1793, stated that as many as 30 ships were engaged in transporting the product to the mainland.

One of the Merchants engaged in this trade was William Watt, major shareholder in the firm William Watt Jnr & Co, who were shipowners, bankers, insurers, ironmongers and drapers. In 1776, the firm owned, or part-owned, the *William*, a sloop of 80 tons, and apparently two other ships. Because of the high demand for ships, William Watt decided that there was enough activity to justify purchasing another one. Shipowning was a risky business, however, because of the heavy losses in northern waters (due to storms and the actions of privateers), and he approached two men to take shares with him in the proposed venture. One, James Stewart, who owned the Estate of Brugh in the Island of Westray and was part owner of several ships, agreed to take half of the 16 shares. The other, William Hewison, a shipmaster aged 33 from Westray, took five, leaving William Watt with three shares.

James Stewart did not take part in the management of the ship, his rôle being that of a supplier of capital. He would have been consulted, however, on any major decisions, such as whether or not to send the ship to the Baltic, and would have taken more than a passing interest in the expenditure incurred and income earned from each voyage. There is one record relating to the sale of cargoes of kelp, which was purchased and sold on behalf of Mr Stewart and Mr Watt, so his interest in the operations of the ship may have been considerable.

William Watt, because of his experience in owning and managing ships, and his extensive business interests, would have acted as managing shareholder, although he held the smallest number of shares. He used the vessel to carry cargoes he owned, benefiting from having transportation to meet the firm's requirements for carrying coal and slate.

William Hewison would be Master of the new ship, and responsible for ensuring that she was always seaworthy, and that cargoes were delivered on time and in good order.

The three men would have met to discuss Mr Watt's proposal and the size of ship that should best serve their purpose. As she would be using small harbours, sometimes beaching in order to load or unload certain cargoes, she could not be too big. The majority of vessels employed in the European and Baltic coasting trade at this time were 40-100 tons, and rigged as sloops, so the choice for the prospective owners was fairly limited.

Their first objective was to find out if there was a ship for sale that would meet their requirements. The most obvious place to look was the port of Leith, the largest, busiest port on the east coast of Scotland, which had had trading links with Orkney for at least 200 years. Mr Watt's ships used the port and one of his business associates, Mr David Balfour, a lawyer, lived in Edinburgh. If it was decided to build a ship in Leith, there were shipbuilders capable of building one to their requirements.

Captain Hewison went to Leith early in 1777, to either buy a ship or have one built to the agreed specifications. In April he wrote to Mr Watt, informing him that no ship was available for sale and he had arranged for one to be built. If the letter was brief it did provide all the essential details; cost of the ship, how many tons of cargo she would carry, and method of payment. Mr Watt and Mr Stewart obviously agreed with the decision, for the *Lloyd's Register* for 1795 records that a sloop of 61 tons, called the *Peggy and Isabella* , was built in 1777, in Leith.

A copy of Captain Hewison's letter is given in Figure 1, with a following transcript, together with an explanation of some of the terms used.

Figure 1

Letter from Hewison to Watt and Stewart, 1777.

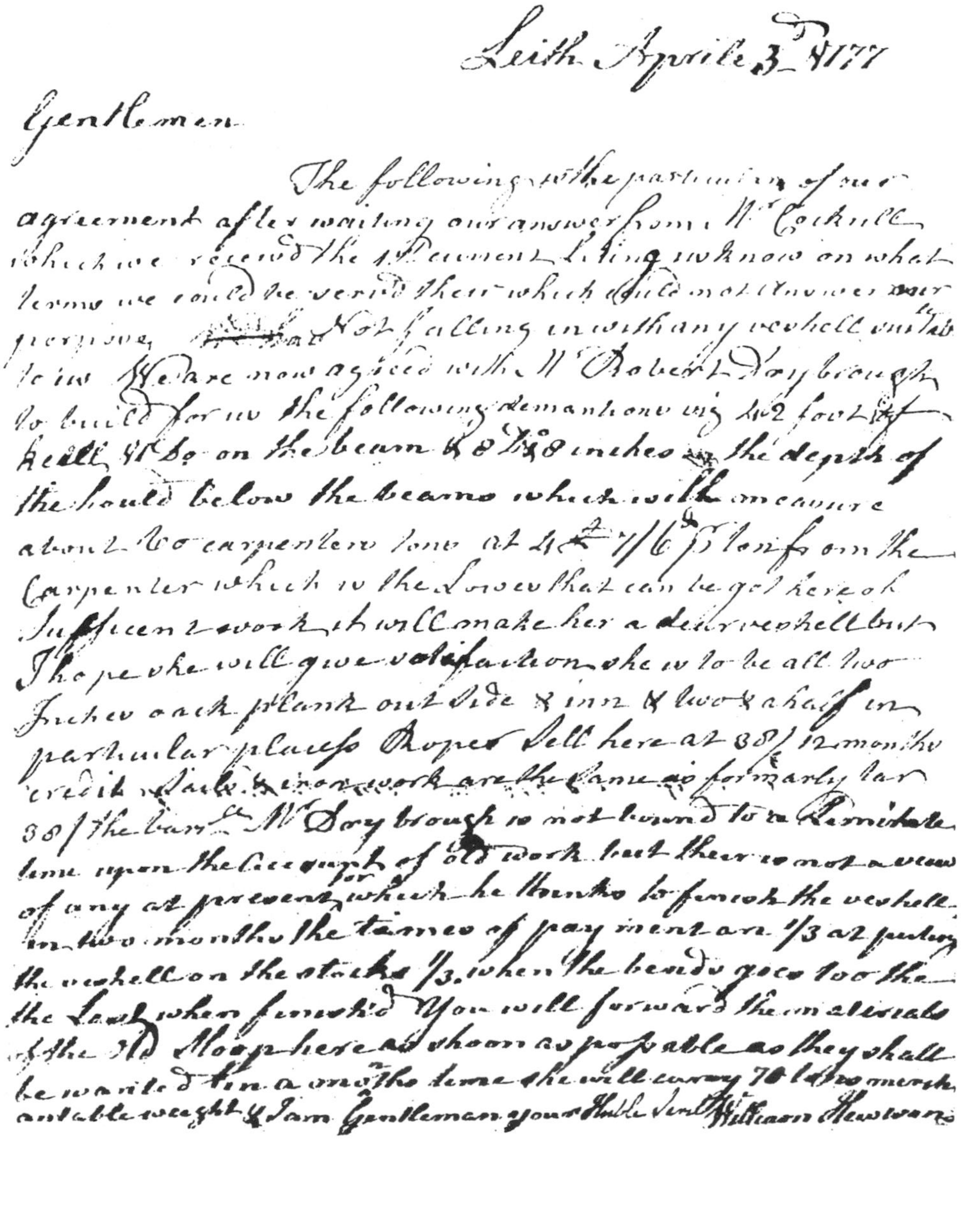

Figure 1, transcript:

Leith, April 3, 1777

Gentlemen,

The following is the particulars of our agreement after waiting our answer from Mr Cockrill which we receivd the 1st current [leting?] us know on what terms we could be servd their which might not answer our perpose. Not falling in with any veshell suitable to us We are now agreed with Mr Robert Drybrough (1) to build for us the following demanshons viz 42 foot of keall & d[itt]o on the beam 8 [foot] 8 inches in the depth of the hould below the beams which will measure about 60 carpentere tons (2) at 4£ 7/ 6 (3) [per] ton (4) from the Carpenter which is the Lowest that can be got here of Sufficient work it will make her a dear veshell but I hope she will give satisfaction she is to be all two Inches oack plank (5) [outside?] 8 inches & two & half in particular placess. Ropes Sell here at 30/- [ ] 12 months with Sails and iron work are the same as formerly tar 30-/- the barr'l. Mr Drybrough is not bound to a Limitede time upon the [ ] of old work but their is not a view of any at present for which he thinks to finish the veshell in two months. The tairms of payment (6) are $^1/_3$ at puting the veshell on the stocks $^1/_3$ when the bends goes [ ] the Last when finish'd. You will forward the materials of the old Sloop[7] here as shoon as possable as they shall be wanted in a months time. She will carry 70 ton (8)[?suit]able weaght.

I am Gentlemen your Hu'le Serv't
William Hewison

Figure 1, explanation of terms:

1. *The Shipbuilder*
There were at least three men in Leith capable of building large ships. One, Robert Dryborough, had had a shipyard in the port since 1754. He gave up business in 1778, so the *Peggy and Isabella* was one of the last ships he built. In Northern Europe, the term used to describe a shipbuilder was *timmerman*, which was still used in Scandinavian countries in this century. The term, used in Leith in the 16th and 17th centuries, was replaced by *carpenter* in the 18th century. (*Carpenter* was used in this way elsewhere in Britain at the time, not only in Leith.) Dryborough was described as a shipbuilder in local records in order to distinguish him from his carpenters. The term *carpenter* was still used in the 19th Century to describe shipwrights working in Leith.

2. *60 Carpenter Tons*
To resolve the difficulty in finding a standard measure for determining tonnage, the Government set out a formula in an Act of 1671, which was amended by further Acts in 1694 and 1720. The method, however, was still open to interpretation, giving rise to significant differences in tonnage for ships with similar dimensions built in different ports. Another formula, set out in an Act of 1773, defined in clear terms the method to be used to calculate tonnage. There was a great need for a standard measure to be used throughout Britain. Tonnage was used by the Government as a basis for hiring ships, by shipbuilders for charging prospective owners, and by Port Authorities for charging vessels for use of the port.

There was no statutory requirement for carpenters or shipowners to use the formula given in the Act of 1773, and carpenters continued to use the method of calculating tonnage which was generally accepted in their port. Different ports varied in the formula used to calculate tonnage of ships and this gave rise to considerable difficulty when ships' tonnage was assessed by the Government Harbour Authorities.

13

The method of calculating tonnage which was set in the 1694 Act was simple to calculate and generally adopted. The reason for its adoption may well have been that it was in general use well before the Act became law. This Act was passed with the intention of raising money and imposed a duty on the tonnage of all ships bringing goods into the country. The formula was as follows:

(Length of keel x breadth x depth) ÷ 94

This method was not satisfactory for two reasons. The keel of a ship can be measured without difficulty if it is in a dock or lying on shore. The Act did not apparently specify if breadth would be taken to mean the external or internal width of a ship. Due to the thickness of timbers used in construction, the difference in external and internal width could result in a significant difference in tonnage. The Act of 1773, which was passed to prevent smuggling, included means of calculating tonnage while a ship was afloat. This particular formula did not involve measuring the depth of the ship. As a result, ships were built which had very deep hulls which enabled them to carry more cargo. This was a period when speed in delivering a cargo did not matter. The important factors as far as a shipowner was concerned, were that the ship should carry as much cargo as possible, and, as the tonnage was based on length and breadth, that the tonnage on which he was charged was kept to a minimum.

Disregarding the issue of depth, the 1773 formula, which was later used in the Registry Act of 1786, did set out a method of calculating tonnage so that men with limited skills would understand the dimensions to be measured and therefore could calculate tonnage.

The 1786 Act formula was very important in that it required all ships to be assessed for tonnage using a standard method and it was applied to all British-owned ships. The formula used in the Acts of 1694, 1773 and 1786, all used the division of 94. This was chosen because it gave a quotient of 56 cubic feet. This was approximately the amount of space occupied in a ship's hold by a wine barrel, known as a tun.

The Victorians were more prosaic in measuring tonnage, as cargoes of wine did not form a large proportion of imports into Britain, and used a division of 3,500 for the formula set out in the Registration Act of 1836, and this figure is used to this day.

In his letter, Hewison gives the length of the keel and the depth of the hull and the breadth, but this last measurement is illegible. As the product of the formula is given as 60, it is possible to determine the breadth as 15 foot 6 inches. The measure of tonnage in *Lloyd's Register* for 1796, is 61, so the final measurements would have differed slightly from the original estimate.

3. *4£7.6*

All the Disbursement Records and statements follow the standard practice, so putting the £ sign after the number was an example of William Hewison's phonetic spelling. Correct spelling (in modern terms) or not, his meaning is always clear.

4. *Cost per ton*

The price quoted by the builder was £4.7.6 per ton. This was the price for the supply of the hull, masts and standing rigging.

Before the ship was ready to sail, the owners would have to spend a considerable amount on sails, installation of running rigging, iron work, fitting out living quarters, anchors, boats, hawsers and other miscellaneous equipment. It was customary for the future Master of the ship to be in the yard whilst she was being built. He ensured that no inferior materials were used in the construction and she was completed according to the agreed specifications. His expenses for attending the shipbuilding, and launch expenses, had to be taken into account.

An example of the work required in fitting out a ship, and the costs incurred, is given in Figure 2. It is for a ship of 40 tons, the *Lady Gray*, built in 1774, by a Dundee

Perth 22d March 1774 Acco Cost of the Sloop Lady Gray built at Dundee. —

Wm Stormonth Carpenters Acco.t —	£ 134	4 3
Roperie Acco.t for Cordages &c —	67	10 10
Murrock & Stewarts Acco. for Canvas. —	29	12 6
Blockmakers Acct —	5	17 1½
Masts. —	16	10 "
Cabin Work —	1	15 "
fitting the Rigging —		6 "
a Norway Log for a Pump —	9	18 2½
a Boat & 2 Anchors —		15 4
a Barrel of Tar & 2 Ankers —	1	1 "
a Main Boom —	3	14 3
Bolsprit Yards & deals —	3	5 2
at Launching the Vessel —		12 6
Ballast —		17 6
Masons for a Stove &c —		6 "
hooks for the Mast —	4	9 2
a Stove Tea Kettle & Tinder Box —	6	10 3
David Myln Charges attending —	4	8 9
Carpenters Allowance for drink —		15 5½
Ditto tools &c —		
Sundry Disbursements by D. Myln for the Vessel when building — }	5	8 1
Altering the Main Sail &c Andrew Morison	4	14 4½
A Clark Smith his Acco —	36	1 9
	319	19 6

Figure 2
Costings for the sloop, *Lady Gray*, 1774. (Reproduced by permission of the National Library of Scotland.)

shipbuilder at a cost of £8.9.6 per ton. David Hynd, whose expenses are entered in the list, was her future Master and part owner. One item of interest on the list is the purchase of a Norway log for use as a pump. Hollowed out, with a piece of leather to provide suction, a shaft and a handle, it would have been an effective and well-used piece of equipment (see below).

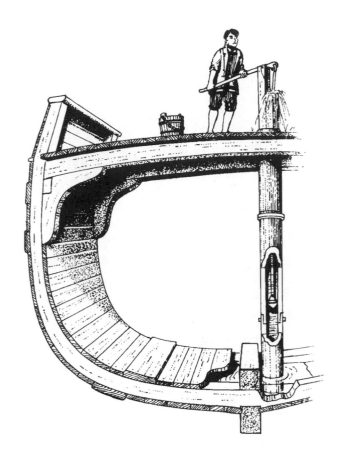

This type of pump would have been installed in the *Peggy and Isabella*. Its diameter would not have been much more than two-three inches, and its power of suction limited as the inside of the pipe would not have been completely circular. All wooden-hulled ships leaked, and there was always sufficient water in the bilges (the lowest part of a ship), to require the crew to operate the pump every day. In bad weather the pump would be able to cope with additional water as long as the hull was in good condition, and this would have been continually checked. It was essential that the pump was well-maintained, and the disbursement records show that a considerable amount of money was spent each year on repair and replacement of various parts of the pump.

Based on these costs, it is possible to estimate the cost of building and fitting out the *Peggy and Isabella*.

	£
Supply of hull masts and standing rigging, (according to Dryborough's estimate of £4.7.6 per ton for a ship of 60 tons)	260
Rigging and sails	130
Smith work	40
Blocks and sundry carpenter work	40
Equipment, boat anchors etc.	30
Sundry expenses	10
Total	510

This would give a cost of £8.4. - equivalent to the cost of similar Scottish ships for this period. The amount would have been reduced if materials and equipment from one of Watt's old ships had been used.

5. Material
The only timber mentioned in the letter is oak for the planks. Because of its strength, oak would have been used to construct the ribs too, and pine, because of its flexibility,

would have been used for the masts and spars. The timber may have come from Scotland, as records exist of oak being supplied from Fife for use in Leith shipyards. It is more likely, however, that most of the timber would have been imported from Norway, which had supplied Leith regularly during the 18th Century. Hemp for the sails, and cordage and tar for sealing the planks, would have been imported from Russia.

6. *Paying for the Ship*

The part of the letter setting out when the instalments would be paid is not very legible. The normal method of payment was: one third when the keel was laid, one third when the bends or ribs were in position, and the balance when the ship was launched.

Shipbuilders had to have a fair amount of working capital to buy materials and pay men after the order had been placed, and before they received the first payment from the owner. They would have carried out repair work in addition to building ships, and this would have helped to ensure that there was enough money to pay for labour and materials. In the 18th Century, Scotland did not have the banking service that developed in the next century, which supplied loans for working capital. The lack of capital meant that few carpenters could expand beyond the building and repair of small boats.

The owners would have had to pay all the other trades over a relatively short period after the vessel was launched. This would not necessarily present a problem to Watt and Stewart, as Watt was a banker in Orkney, and Stewart was known to be a man of substance capable of obtaining a loan if necessary. Hewison would have to find approximately £160, a considerable sum for a young shipmaster.

7. *Materials of the sloop*

It was the practice in these days for materials which were in good working order to be taken from ships which had reached the end of their working life and used on new ships in order to reduce costs. William Hewison did not specify the "materials" in his letter. Only new timber would be used for the hull and deck, so it is likely that recently renewed spars, hatch covers and boats would have been provided for the new ship.

There are many instances in the records where Mr Watt and William Hewison are shown to be thrifty men by using old materials and carrying out repairs rather than incurring expenditure on new equipment. The fact that the old material would contrast unfavourably with the new timber supplied by the carpenter would not have bothered them.

8. *Cargo carrying capacity*

William Hewison stated that the vessel would carry 70 tons, and this was the most important measurement as far as the owners were concerned, not the tonnage figure obtained from the Carpenter's Measure, whch was a measure of capacity and was described as the *tonnage burthen*. This measure was initially used to determine the cost of a ship, but owners were more concerned about the maximum weight which the vessel could carry, and the measure was known as the *deadweight tonnage*. Too large a deadweight tonnage and a large crew would be required and space would be wasted. Too small, and cargoes and incomes would be limited.

The method of determining deadweight tonnage of a ship was to add one third to the tonnage burthen, which, in the case of the *Peggy and Isabella* would have given a figure of 80 tons. Hewison was being careful when he stated that the ship would carry 70 tons, for on several occasions she had cargoes of 77 tons (so the crude measure was reasonably accurate). The majority of her cargoes was well below this figure, but this would have been due to a lack of available cargoes rather than an inability to carry cargoes of between 70-80 tons.

THE RIG OF THE *PEGGY AND ISABELLA*

According to the entries in *Lloyd's Register,* the vessel was rigged as a sloop, which was the usual rig for vessels of between 40-100 tons in the 18th century. A sloop was a single masted vessel described as being rigged fore and aft (with its sails in line with its keel), and it differed from the schooner in having only one mast. This sail arrangement meant that the vessel could use the wind coming from either side and could thus sail close to the wind. The main advantage that a sloop had over square rigged vessels (ships with sails at right angles to the line of the keel), was that the sails were relatively easy to handle. The ships required only a small crew, a Master and two men, and were economical to operate.

Scotland during the 18th century had very few harbours with quays, and ships had to load and discharge their cargoes on beaches and small harbours which dried out at low tide. So that the vessel stayed forcibly upright when on the beach, it had to have a hull with a square cross section. Masters had to be careful that they beached their ship on a good level surface to avoid straining the hull, which could be done if rocks projected above the surface of the harbour or beach.

The lines of a typical 18th century sloop are given in Figure 3, and these show a vessel which had a high ratio of beam to length, and a flat floor. Its wide beam meant that it had a good cargo carrying capacity, and its flat floor allowed the vessel to stay upright in a dried-out harbour. Another characteristic of its hull was its well-rounded or bluff bows. It was standard practice to build ships with bluff bows at this time, and it would be another 50 years before builders of merchant ships started to adopt the clipper or sharp bow.

Whilst shippers required their cargoes to be delivered in reasonable time, speed was not necessarily too important, and the sloop's square-shaped hull and round bows were not seen as a disadvantage. The important requirement was for the cargo to be delivered in good condition, and a Master's reputation depended upon the ability to deliver his cargoes safely and expeditiously.

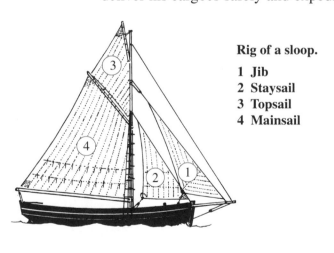

Rig of a sloop.

1 Jib
2 Staysail
3 Topsail
4 Mainsail

By the time of the last recorded entry in *Lloyd's Register* in 1807, the rig of the *Peggy and Isabella* was out of fashion. Although the sloop rig was effective for small vessels, the large mainsail was not only difficult to handle itself, it also made the ship awkward to handle in confined waters. By the end of the 18th century, the Dutch were increasingly using the schooner rig, with two masts and smaller sails, which were easier to handle. The sloop rig was still used in the 19th century, but increasingly, small ships of between 60-150 tons, were rigged as topsail schooners. These vessels still had the fore and aft rig, but also had two small squaresails on the mainmast which gave the vessel considerable manoeuvrability.

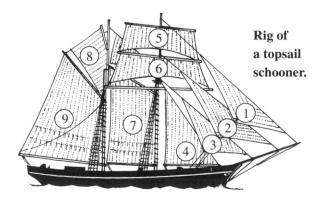

Rig of a topsail schooner.

1 Flying jib   2 Outer jib   3 Inner jib
4 Fore staysail   5 Fore upper topsail
6 Fore lower topsail   7 Foresail
8 Gaff topsail   9 Mainsail

LINES OF AN 18TH CENTURY SLOOP

Figure 3
**The sloop
Clio. Drawn
by David R
MacGregor,
(from a plan
found in
Whitby
Museum).**

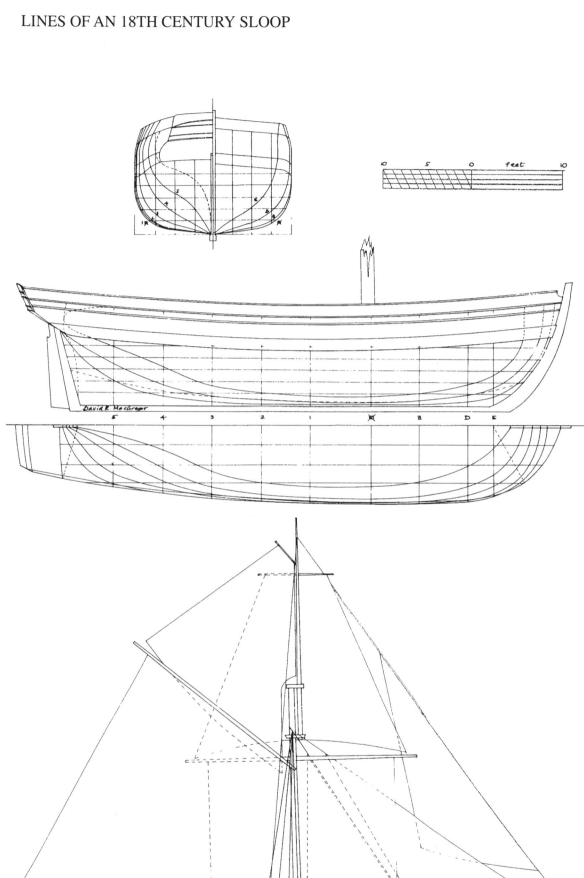

OFFER TO BUILD

Hewison's letter sets out the specifications of the ship which Robert Drybrough and he agreed should be built. This letter appears to be the only record of the transaction. The normal practice was for a shipbuilder to make a formal offer in writing to the prospective shipowner, giving details of the dimensions, materials to be used and terms of payment. No doubt Hewison, because of his experience as a Master, and in his capacity as a shareholder, was empowered to act on behalf of Messrs Watt and Stewart, and reached an agreement with Dryborough without the formal written offer. If such a written offer had been made, it would have been couched in similar terms to that made by another Leith shipbuilder, John Willison, in 1765, to William Watt. A copy of this letter

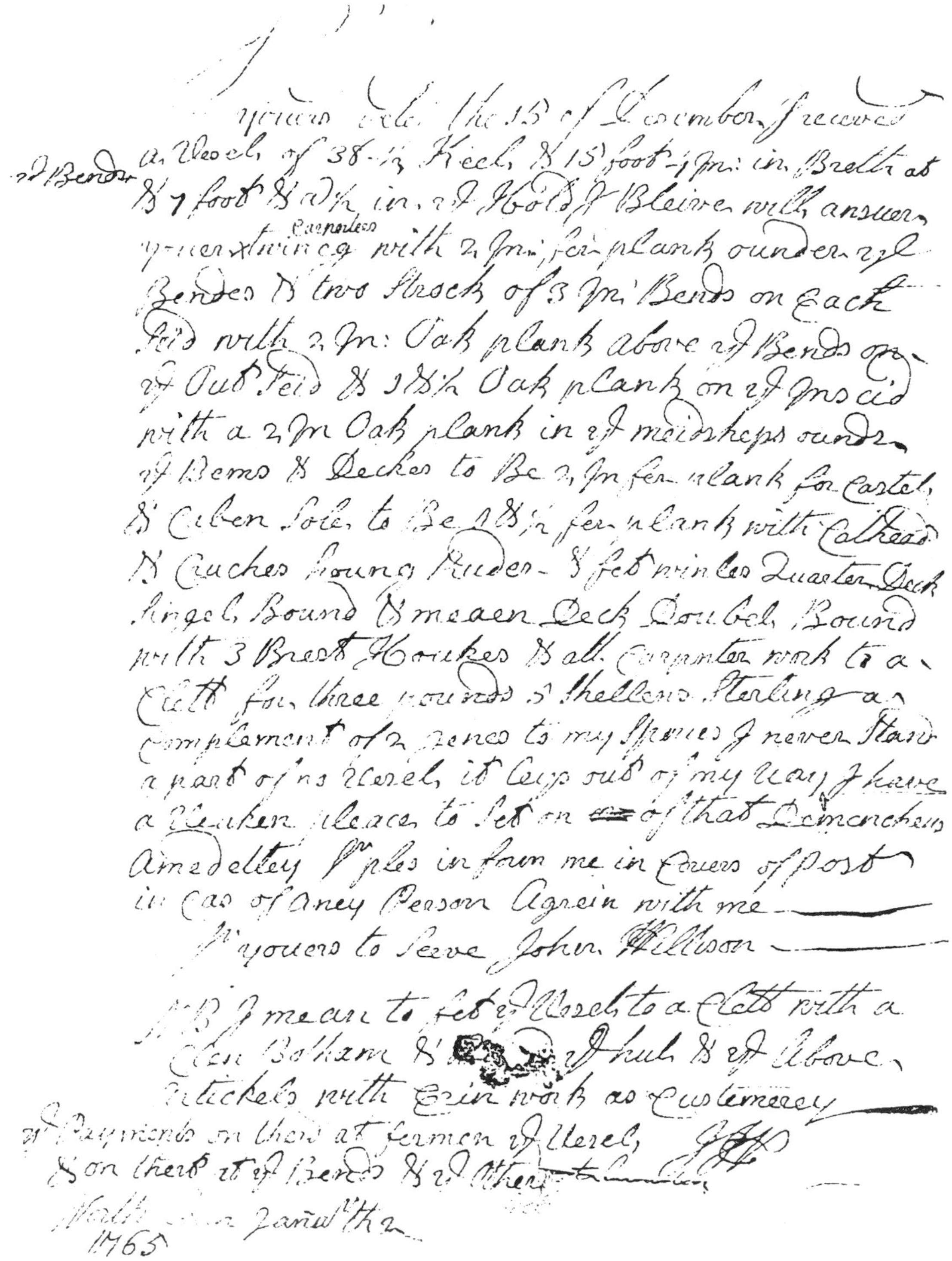

yours dele the 13 of December I received
a Vesel of 38 1/2 Keel & 15 foot 4 In: in Breth at Bends
& 7 foot & a 1/2 in. ye Hold I Bleive will answer
your Carpenters Drawing with 2 In: fer plank ounder ye
Bendes & two Strock of 3 In: Bends on Each
Seid with 2 In: Oak plank above ye Bends on
ye Out Seid & 1 1/2 Oak plank on ye Inseid
with a 2 In Oak plank in ye meidships ounder
ye Bems & Deckes to Be 2 In fer plank for Castel
& Ciben Sole to Be 1 1/2 In fer plank with Catheads
& Cuches hound Ruder & Sed winles Quarter Deck
Angel Bound & meaen Deck Doubel Bound
with 3 Brest Hoockes & all Carpenter work to a
Clett for three pounds 5 Shellens Sterling a
Complement of 2 Pences to my Sprices I never Stand
a part of ns Vesel it Leys out of my way I have
a Beaken pleace to set on of that Demenchen
Amedeltey pleas in form me in Course of Post
in Cas of Aney Person Agrein with me
Yours to Serve John Willison

N.B. I mean to set ye Vesel to a Clett with a
Clen Bottom & ye hul & ye Above
Articles with Erin work as Customeray
ye Payments on thed at Fermen ye Vesel
& on thed at ye Bends & ye other
Leith Janu 7th 2
1765

Figure 4
Letter from Willison to Watt, 1765.

is given in Figure 4, together with an explanation of the terms used. Based on the dimensions given, this would be for a vessel of 43 tons, and it is possible that Willison's offer is for the sloop, *William*, which was built in 1765/6. No record of the *William* appears on Lloyd's Register for this period, so it is not possible to ascertain the tonnage of this ship. Disbursement records of the *William*, indicate that it was a small ship of not more than 40/50 tons.

The Watt papers contain a statement of expenditure incurred in the fitting out of the *William*, and this was prepared because one of the four shareholders, possibly Mr Watt, objected to the expenditure incurred by a James Fotheringham, who owned a quarter share in the ship, and who apparently supervised the construction and fitting out of the sloop. The majority of the expenditure on the ship was accepted by Mr Watt, and the dispute was about the sum of £54.2.1/2, which Watt claimed had already been paid by him to certain tradesmen.

The document is very detailed and interesting in that it shows that William Watt, acting on behalf of the other two shareholders, maintained not only a careful record of the work carried out by all tradesmen, but also the payments made to the men.

Fotheringham seems to have been ignorant of the completeness of Watt's record, and tried to claim for expenditure already incurred. Unfortunately, no records exist to show if Fotheringham became Master of the *William*.

From an examination of the statement which is dated 1767, it would appear that the ship was built by James Donaldson, another Leith shipbuilder, so that Willison's offer, dated 1765, was not accepted.

Figure 4, transcript:
Sir, youers date. the 15th of December I received. A Vesel of 38 1/3 [foot] Keel, & 15 foot 4 In[che]s in Breth at the Bends(1) *& 7 foot & a 1/2 in the Hold I bleive will ansuer youer carpenter's turn* [purpose] *eg with 2 in fer plank ounder the Bendes & two strock of 3 in Bends on Each seid, with 2 in Oak plank above the Bends on the Out seid, and 1 1/2 [in] Oak plank on the Inseid, with a 2 in Oak plank in the meidships ounder the Bems and Deckes to Be 1 In fer plank for Castel and Caben soles* [decks] *to Be 1 1/2 [in] fer plank, with Cathead & Cruches houng Ruder* (2) *- and fit winles* [windlass]. *Quarter Deck Singel Bound and meaen* [main] *Deck Doubel Bound, with three Brest Houkes* [breasthooks] *& all Carpenter work to a Clett* (3), *for three pounds 5 Shellens Sterling* [per ton] *an complement of 2 genes* [guineas] *to my Spoues* (4). *I never Stand a part of no Vesel, it leys out of my Way* (5). *I have a veaken pleace* [vacant place] *to Set on of that Demenchens Amedelty [immediately] S'r, ples inform me in Couers of Post, in Cas of Aney* [other] *Person agrein* [agreeing] *with me.*
Sir, youers to Serve, John Willison

An 18th century wooden windlass.

NB I mean to [?out]*fit the Vesel to a Clett, with a Clen Botham* [clean bottom], *& [?provide] the hul & the Above Artickels with Erin* [iron] *work as custimerey. The Payments, on* [one] *therd at fermen* [forming] *the vesel & on therd at the Bends, and the Other [ ].*
North Leith, [ ] [January 2], *1765.*

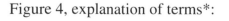

Figure 4, explanation of terms*:

1. *Bends*
This term has been taken as referring to the ribs of the vessel. From the lines of the vessel, it can be seen that the ribs were curved and took a considerable amount of time and skill to complete.

21

* I am grateful to Mrs Sue Mowatt, FSA Scotland, for advice on the meaning of certain terms used by John Willison.

2. *Cathead-and-crutches hung rudder*

The cathead was a term for the sternpost which was fixed to the keel and to which was attached the rudder. Crutches were iron pieces which fastened the rudder to the cathead or sternpost.

3. *Clett*

This term does not appear in the older Scottish dictionaries and it appears to mean a finish, or standard, so that other tradesmen, such as sailmakers, blacksmiths and carpenters, can do their work and make the vessel ready to sail.

4. *Complement of 2 guineas to my spouse*

It was accepted practice in the 17th and 18th centuries for a payment to be made to the builder's wife.

5. *I never stand a part of no vessel, it lies out of my way*

Some shipbuilders accepted a share in a ship as part payment. Willison, however, did not accept the practice.

SHIPPING RECORDS

The only record of ships owned by Scots in the 18th century are Customs registers of exports and imports for the latter half of the 18th century, and Admiralty Court Records. These sources provide, in some cases, the home port of a vessel, the names of its Master and owner(s), and, very occasionally, the tonnage of the vessel.

To collect information about the British Merchant Fleet, an Act of Parliament was passed in 1786, which required details of all British-owned, and built, ships over 15 tons to be recorded on registers, and Customs Officers to be maintained at specified ports throughout Britain. The registers contained details of the rig, number of decks and masts, figurehead, hull dimensions and tonnage of a ship. There was also provision for changes in hull dimensions and tonnage. The names of the Master and owner(s) were also recorded, as well as the number of shares held by individual owners. With this information, it was possible to check if a vessel was sailing under an assumed name, which sometimes happened in that part of the 18th century, when so many vessels were engaged in smuggling.

These shipping registers were maintained by Customs Officers in Kirkwall, and the *Peggy and Isabella,* along with other ships, would have registered in that port. Her owners would have been given a Certificate of Registry, which had to be carried on board the vessel and produced when required by Government port officials. Later Acts of Registry made the registry itself the repository of title, and the certificate became less important, although it still had to be carried on board the ship.

A copy of the Certificate of Registry of the *Barbara and Ann,* which was issued in Banff in 1816, is given in Figure 5. This document gives all the relevant information to allow the vessel to be identified. Such a register would have provided all the important details about the *Peggy and Isabella,* and the various owners that she had during her lifetime. Sadly, registers for the period do not exist, and details of the ship and her owners are, to some extent, a matter for conjecture.

In the 18th, and early part of the 19th, centuries, many British ships were captured by privateers, who took the Registry Certificate and used it for a foreign-owned vessel to obtain the privileges accorded to a British ship, such as carrying British goods. If a vessel was captured or lost, the Master had to produce a statement explaining the circumstances which led to the loss of the Certificate of Registry, and the register recorded the nature of the loss. A declaration of the loss of the Certificate of Registry in a

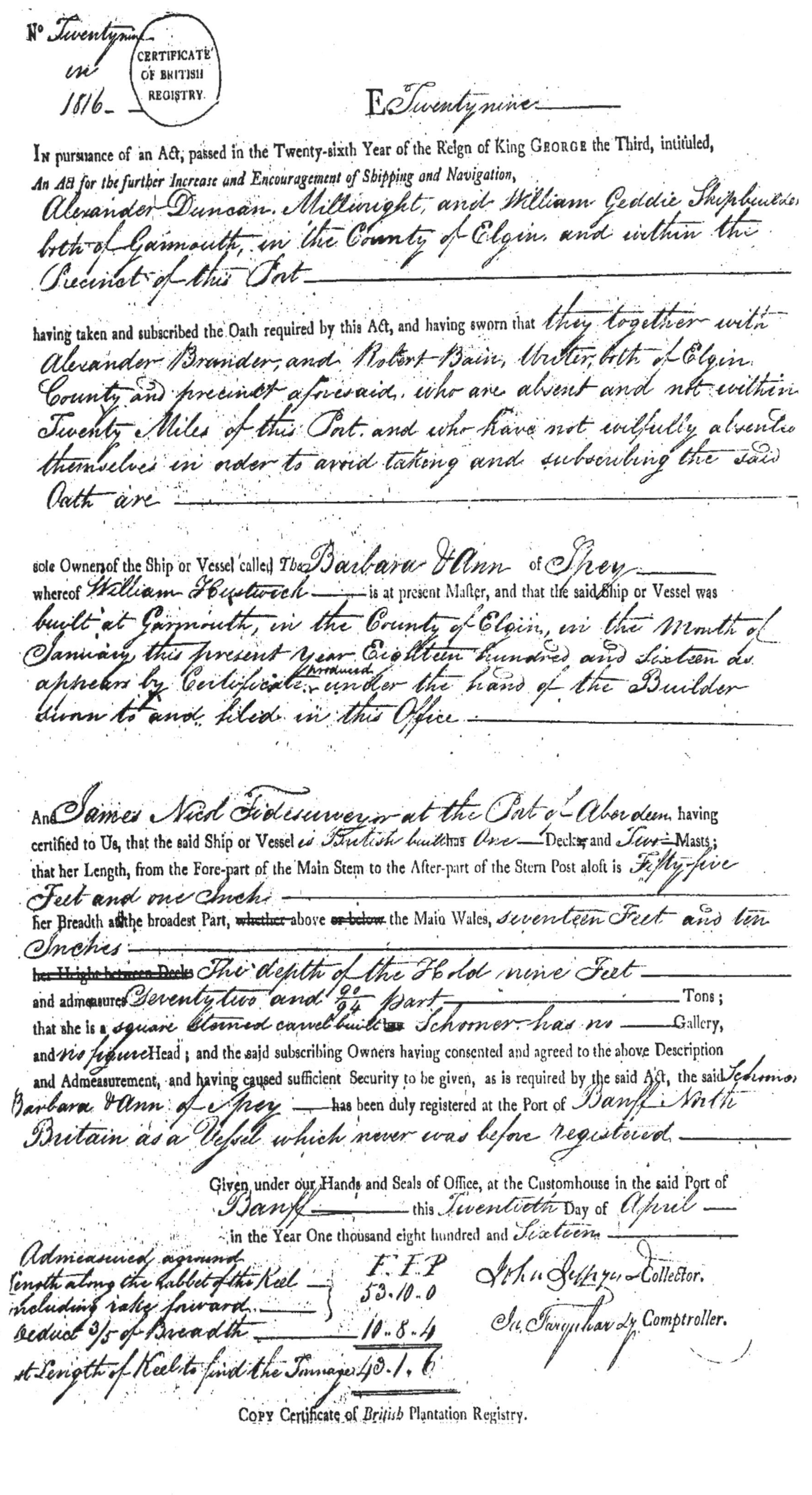

Figure 5
Certificate of Registry of the *Barbara and Ann*, 1816.

Nº Twenty-nine
in
1816 —

CERTIFICATE OF BRITISH REGISTRY.

E Twenty nine —

In pursuance of an Act, passed in the Twenty-sixth Year of the Reign of King GEORGE the Third, intituled, An Act for the further Increase and Encouragement of Shipping and Navigation,

Alexander Duncan. Millwright, and William Geddie Shipbuilder, both of Garmouth, in the County of Elgin. and within the Precinct of this Port —

having taken and subscribed the Oath required by this Act, and having sworn that *they together with Alexander Brander, and Robert Bain, Writer, both of Elgin County and precinct aforesaid, who are absent and not within Twenty Miles of this Port. and who have not wilfully absented themselves in order to avoid taking and subscribing the said Oath are* —

sole Owner of the Ship or Vessel called The *Barbara & Ann — of Spey* — whereof *William Kirstwick* — is at present Master, and that the said Ship or Vessel was *built at Garmouth, in the County of Elgin, in the Month of January this present Year Eighteen hundred and Sixteen as appears by Certificate produced under the hand of the Builder Sworn to and filed in this Office* —

And *James Nicol Tidesurveyor at the Port of Aberdeen*, having certified to Us, that the said Ship or Vessel *is British built* has One — Deck and Two — Masts; that her Length, from the Fore-part of the Main Stem to the After-part of the Stern Post aloft is *Fifty-five Feet and one Inch* — her Breadth at the broadest Part, whether above or below the Main Wales, *seventeen Feet and ten Inches* — her Height between Decks *The depth of the Hold nine Feet* — and admeasures *Seventy two and 90/94 Part* — Tons; that she is a square Sterned carvel built *Schooner* has no — Gallery, and no figure Head; and the said subscribing Owners having consented and agreed to the above Description and Admeasurement, and having caused sufficient Security to be given, as is required by the said Act, the said *Schooner Barbara & Ann of Spey* — has been duly registered at the Port of *Banff North Britain as a Vessel which never was before registered* —

Given under our Hands and Seals of Office, at the Customhouse in the said Port of *Banff* — this *Twentieth* Day of *April* — in the Year One thousand eight hundred and *Sixteen* —

Admeasured around
Length along the Rabbet of the Keel
including rake forward. — F.F.P 53.10.0
deduct 3/5 of Breadth — 10.8.4
at Length of Keel to find the Tonnage 43.1.6

John Jeffrey Collector.
Ja. Farquhar Jr Comptroller.

COPY Certificate of British Plantation Registry.

23

Port of Inverness.

Figure 6
**Declaration
of loss of
Certificate
of Registry,
1852.**

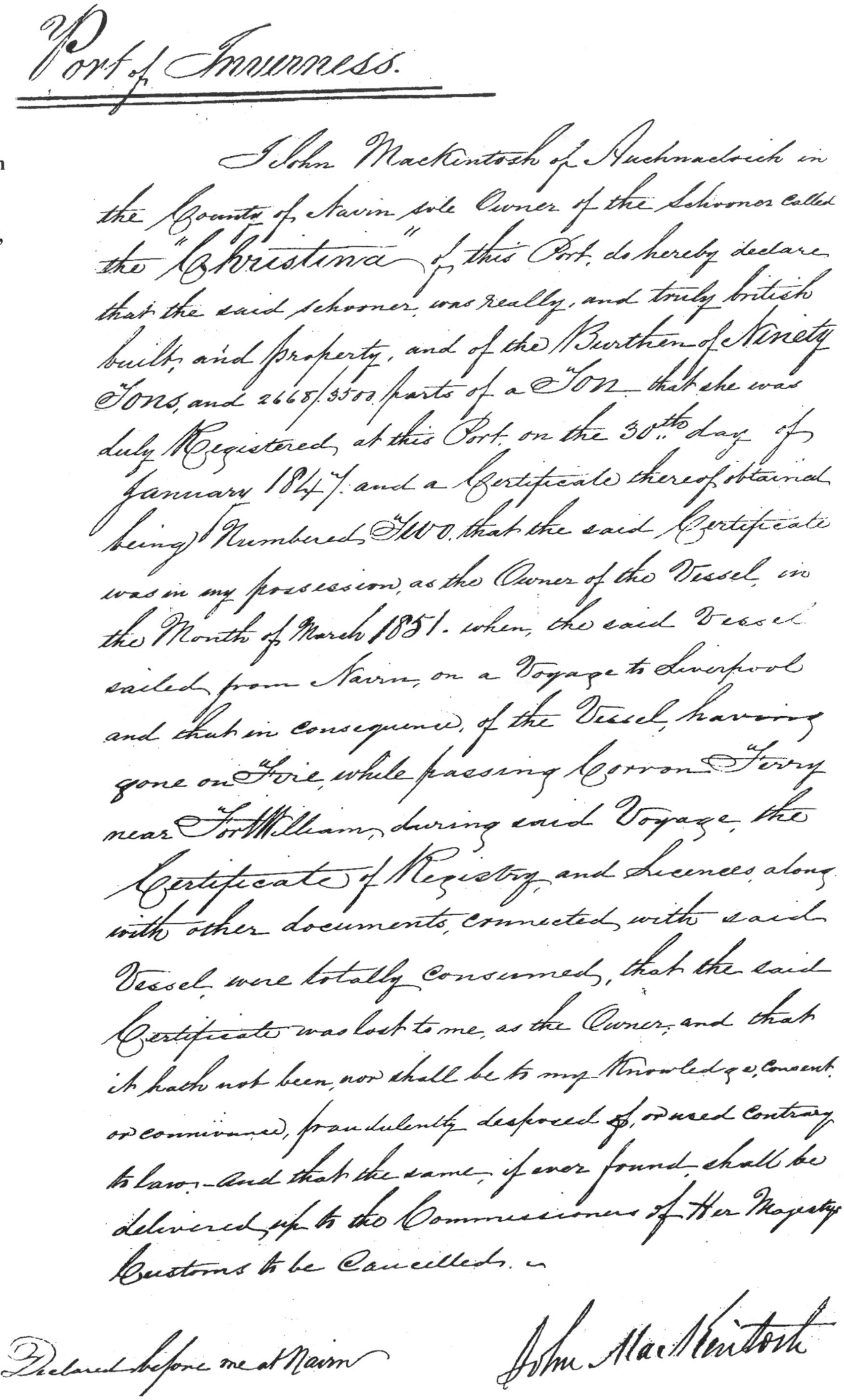

I John MacKintosh of Auchnacloich in the County of Nairn sole Owner of the Schooner called the "Christina" of this Port, do hereby declare that the said schooner, was really, and truly british built, and property, and of the Burthen of Ninety Tons, and 2668/3500 parts of a Ton that she was duly Registered, at this Port, on the 30.th day of January 1847. and a Certificate thereof obtained being Numbered Two. that the said Certificate was in my possession, as the Owner of the Vessel, in the Month of March 1851. when, the said Vessel sailed from Nairn, on a Voyage to Liverpool and that in consequence, of the Vessel, having gone on Fire, while passing Corran Ferry near Fort William, during said Voyage, the Certificate of Registry, and Licences, along with, other documents, connected, with said Vessel, were totally consumed, that the said Certificate was lost to me, as the Owner; and that it hath not been, nor shall be to my Knowledge, consent, or connivance, fraudulently disposed of, or used contrary to law.—And that the same, if ever found, shall be delivered up to the Commissioners of Her Majesty Customs to be Cancelled.

Declared before me at Nairn

John MacKintosh

fire aboard the schooner *Christina*, is given in Figure 6.

When the *Pomona*, a vessel owned in part by William Watt, and commanded by William Hewison, was captured by the French in 1796, the Customs wrote to the brother of the owner, Colonel Balfour, requesting a report on the vessel's capture. A copy of this letter is given in Figure 7.

When a vessel was captured, the event was recorded in *Lloyd's List* which was issued several times a month, and an extract from the Marine List for March 3, 1796, given in Figure 8, provides details of ships captured by the Navy, and British ships taken by privateers.

The only list of ships available in the latter part of the 18th century, was that provided by *Lloyd's Register of Shipping*, which first appeared in 1764, and included details of some 4,500 vessels. These early registers were published at intervals of two to three years, and it was not until the 1770's that they were published annually. There was a good reason for a shipowner paying a fee to have his vessel surveyed and the details entered in the register. Prospective consignors of goods by sea could ascertain the vessel's tonnage, age and draught of water when loaded. In some cases, the type of timber used in her construction, and when she was last surveyed, would be entered.

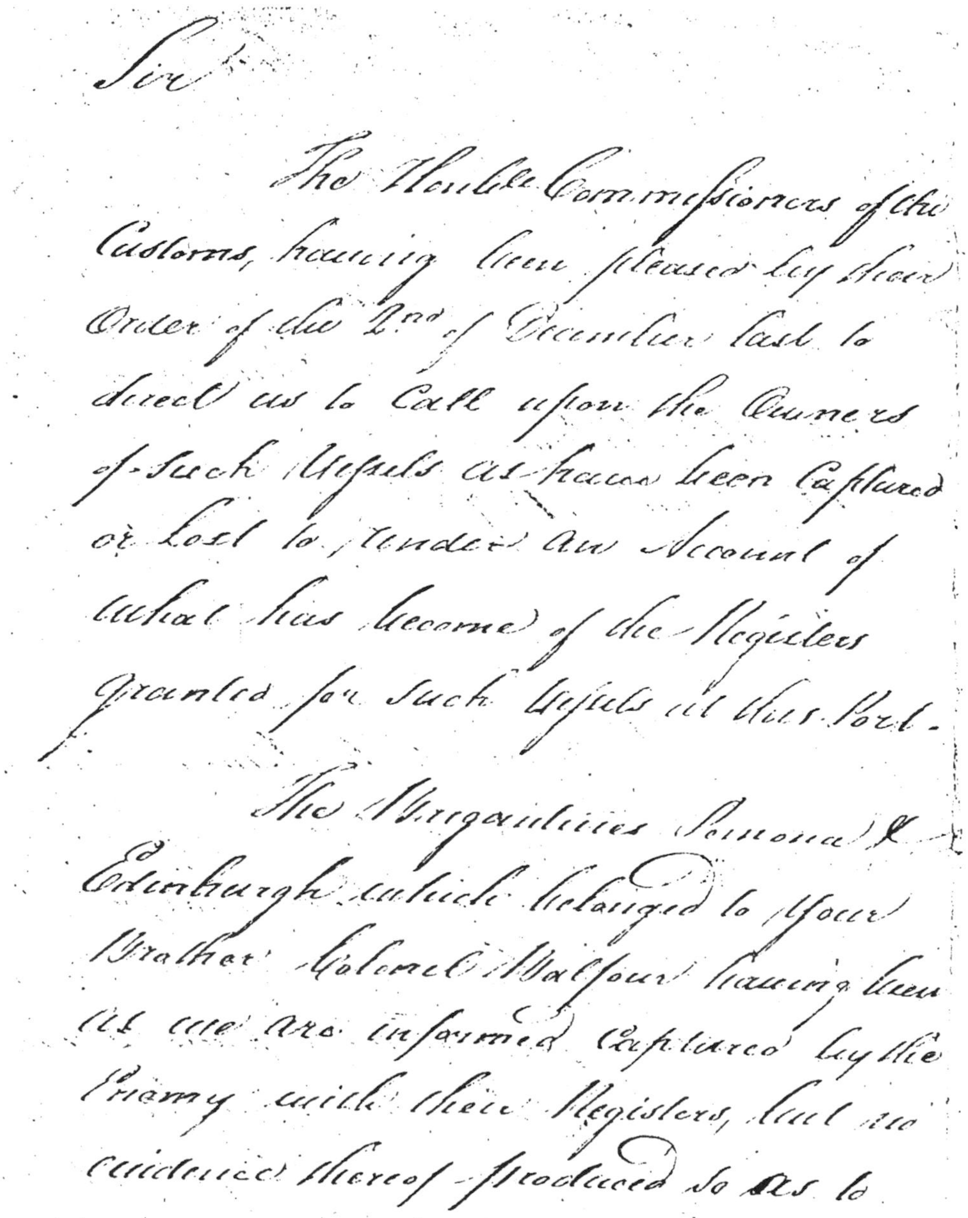

Figure 7
Letter from Kirkwall Customs, 1807.

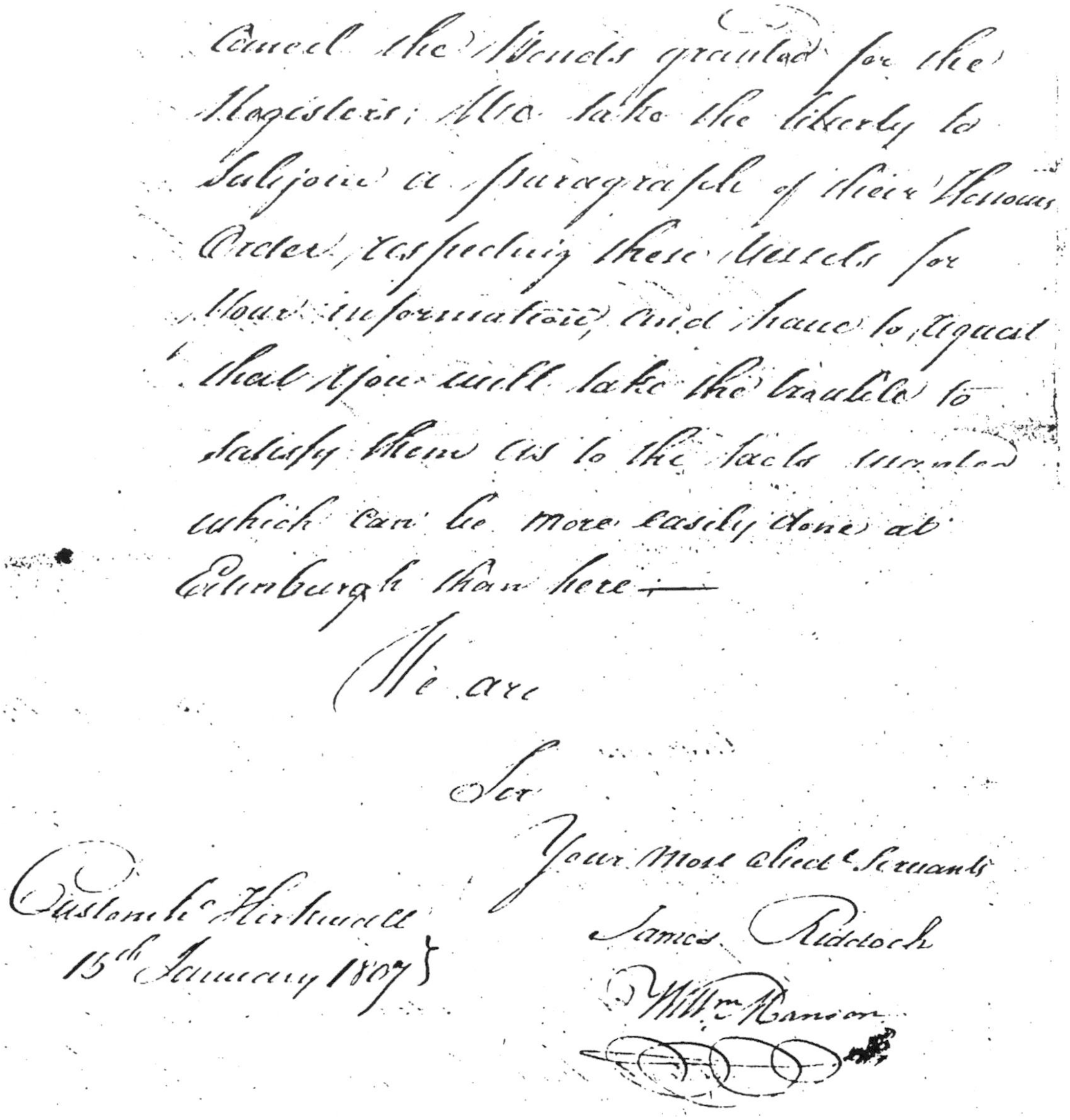
Cancel the Bonds granted for the
Registers; Also take the liberty to
Subjoin a paragraph of their Honours
Order, respecting these Vessels for
Your information, and have to request
that You will take the trouble to
satisfy them as to the facts wanted
which can be more easily done at
Edinburgh than here—

We are

Sir

Your Most obed.t Servants

James Riddoch

Will.m Manson

Custom h.e Kirkwall
15th January 1807

Figure 7, transcript:

Sir

The Honb'le Commissioners of the Customs, having been pleased by their order of the 2nd of December last to direct us to call upon the Owners of such Vessels as have been Captured or Lost to render an Account of what has become of the Registers granted for such Vessels at this Port.

The Brigantine Pomona of Edinburgh which belonged to your brother Colonel Balfour having been as we are informed Captured by the Enemy with their Registers, but no guidance thereof produced so as to cancel the bonds granted for the Registers; We take the liberty to Subjoin a paragraph of their Honours Order respecting these vessels for your information, and have to request that you will take the trouble to satisfy them as to the facts wanted which can be more easily done at Edinburgh than here-

We are

Sir

Your most obed't servants

Custom h'e[house] *Kirkwall* — *James Riddoch*

15th January 1807 — *Wll'm Manson*

A copy of the page in *Lloyd's Register* for 1797, together with the page that explains the abbreviations used in the register (Figure 8, reproduced overleaf), show the entry for the *Peggy and Isabella*, which provided some information on the ship, although not as much as entries in the 19th century registers. The first column gave the name of the ship and her rig, *Sp* being the abbreviation for sloop, *s* for ship and *Bg* for Brig. All other issues of the register give the name *Isabella*, but, for some reason it was shortened here to *Isabel*. The second and third columns give the name of the Master, her tonnage and number of decks. (The Master's name was very important in an age when so much depended upon his experience.) The port where the vessel was built, and when she was built, is given in the 4th and 5th columns. (*Lloyd's* did not recognise Scottish ports other than Leith, Aberdeen and Dundee, and this made it very difficult to determine where a ship was built.)

The next three columns gave the owner's name, the depth of water taken by the ship when fully loaded and her trading area. The name of the owner was as important as the Master's, as a competent owner would ensure the vessel was well maintained and employ good men. The last column gave the classification of the standard of building of the hull. This was only given after a surveyor had examined the ship and any repairs had been carried out. There were five classifications given in that period, *A E I O U*, with *A* being the highest. The *Peggy and Isabella* was in the second grade of *E,* which did not mean she did not have a sound hull, but reflected, in part, the quality of the timbers used, and the hull's age. The figure *95* in this column is the year when the vessel was last surveyed.

From this information, a prospective consignor of goods would have ascertained that the ship had sufficient cargo capacity, and was in good condition as she had been surveyed two years before. From the abbreviation *Lh Orkn*, he would know that she traded mainly between Leith and Orkney.

Although the *Peggy and Isabella* was not surveyed until 1795, merchants using her over the 18 year period since she was built would have known the ship and her Master, and, on a personal basis, would have been satisfied that their cargoes would be carried in a well found ship.

Figure 8
Lloyd's List,
March 3, 1797.
(By permission
of Lloyd's
Register of
Shipping.)

LLOYD's LIST.

No. 2903] LONDON, FRIDAY, MARCH 3, 1797.

THE MARINE LIST.

Captain Calder, arrived this Morning at the Admiralty, with Difpatches from Admiral Sir John Jarvis, giving an Account of his having, on the 14th Ult. fallen in with the Spanifh Fleet, confifting of twenty-feven Sail of the Line, and nine Frigates, off Cape St. Vincent's, and had captured the
Sal de Munde, of 112 Guns;
St. Jofeph, of 112 ditto;
St. Nicholas, of 84 ditto;
St. Efedro, of 74 ditto;
and fix Tranfports, with Ordnance. The Lofs of the Britifh Squadron, confifting of fifteen Sail of the Line, and four Frigates, has been inconfiderable.

By a Letter from Bergen, the following Ships of War are equipping between that Place and Chriftianfand, and nearly ready for Sea: the Venus Dutch Frigate; Scipio ditto ditto; Waaghals ditto Brig; and Vlughver ditto Cutter. The Vengeance French Frigate, of 16 Guns; Syrene Lugger, and Petite Diable Cutter Privateers.

The Sarah, late Curry, from Liverpool to Martinico, recaptured by the Stag Frigate, has been taken again by a French Cutter, and retaken by the fame Frigate, and fent for Portfmouth.

The Hypocrite French Privateer, from Havre, is taken by the Unity Frigate, and fent into Plymouth.

The Maria Privateer, of 6 Guns and 68 Men, from Marfeilles, is taken by the Minerva Frigate.

Le Victoreux Privateer, of 4 Guns, from Dunkirk, is taken by the Leopard.

The Corfo, Spanifh Brig of 18 Guns, and 136 Men, bound from Genoa to Barcelona, is taken by the Southampton Frigate.

L'Adventure Privateer, from Dunkirk, is taken by the Swift Cutter, and carried into Dover.

The Fortuna, Kock, from Barcelona to London, was loft on the Coaft of Portugal the 14th December laft.

The Charlotte, Dannberg, from Barcelona to Cette, is loft, the Crew faved.

The Calypfo, Beard, from Labradore to a Market, was taken in December laft, by Les Droits d'Hommes, French Man of War.— The Crew landed at Breft.

The *Marine List*
referring to the
capture of the
Pomona.

The Hare, Haley, from London to New York, is taken by a fmall Privateer, and carried into Dieppe.

The True Britton, Greaves, from Lifbon to Viana, is taken by a Spanifh Privateer and carried into Vigo.

The Pomona Tranfport, from Gibraltar, is taken and carried into Dieppe.

The Neptune Tranfport, Capt. Green, from Gibraltar, is taken and carried into Bourdeaux.

The Peggy, Bruce, from London to Limerick, is taken by the Ferrett French Privateer.

The Nymph, Houfe, from Naples to London, is taken by Two French Frigates and carried into France; the Frigates are arrived at Conftantinople.

The Three Neighbours, Delday, from Portfmouth to Martinico, is taken and carried into Bourdeaux.

The Commerce, Langlois; and the Queen, Aubin, from Labradore, are taken in the Streights of Gibraltar, and carried into Algeziras. The former is condemned.

The Judith, Young, from Gibraltar to London, is taken and carried into Rochelle.

The Hercules, Hales, from London to the Southern Fifhery, is taken and carried into Bourdeaux.

Left: The page
from *Lloyd's*
Register of
Shipping,
referring to
the *Peggy and*
Isabella.

Right: The
abbreviations
used in the
register.

120	Peggy	Bg	A.Watfor	101	Scotl'd	84	Reid &Co	10	ArkglLh	E 2		
7	—	Bg s	Whitaw	87	Amer.	73	N.Mudge	12	ExOprtc	E 1		E 1
8	—	Bg s	E.Ward	167	falem	92	Salem	12	LiVirgn	E 1		
9	—	Sp	W.Young	56	Scotl'd	77	J.Kidd	8	Lh Nrwy	E 1		
150	—Begbie	Sp	W Nicho	49	Leith	90	Nichol &c	8	Lh	A 1		
1	—&Chriftian	Sp	D.Mourie	62	Ely	94	Capt.	9	Lh	A 1		
2	—&Ifabel	Sp	J Hewifon	61	Leith	77	J.Stewart	9	LhOrkn	E 1		?
3	—&Mary	Sp	T.Jones	50	Wales	87	Capt.&C.	8	Lo.Cork	A 1		
4	—&Sally	Bg	A.Rofs	62	Shmtn	79	Rofs&Co	9	Be Derry	E 1		
5	Peggys	Bg	Atkinfon	107	Scotl'd	92	Capt.&C.	11	LiBelfaft	A 1		
6	—Succefs	S	Henderfn	337	Sndrld	83	R Mordey	15	Br. Cork	E 1		
7	Pelican	Bg	W. Laws	122	Yrmth	95	Vale &Co	10	YaBaltic	A 1		
8	—	Bg	Tronquift	200	Swedn	69	Aberfteen	14	Lo.	E 1		
9	Penelope	S s	Brown	270	Mryld	73	Old & Co.	16	LoStVin	E 1		
140	—	S	Bunker	206	NYork	94	Capt.&C.	13	DuNYrk	A 1		
1	—	Sw s	J.Dafh	124	Scotld	36	Blake&C.	12	FaPlym.	A 1		F
2	—	Sp	J.Morgan	53	Irifh	83	S. Fegan	9	Co Lifbn	E 1		
3	—	Bg	Ormandy	107	Britifh	70	Capt.&C.	10	WnIrlnd	E 1		
4	—	S s	Richmnd	160	Scrbro	81	J.Jackfon	15	PhFerrol	E 1		E 1
5	—	Bg	Sidgwrth	127	Britifh	56	J.Addifon	10	LoPtrfbg	A 1		
6	—	S s.W&C	H.Sphinx	300	French	38	Willis&C	15	LeJamai	A 1		
7	Pennfylvania	S	Harding	287	Philad	92	Pennfylva	15	LiPhilad	A 1		
8	Penrofe	Sp	Mahoney	54	Cork	92	Mahoney	9	CoQ'brn	A 1		
9	Penzance	Sp	J. Quick	67	Bdefrd	85	Oxenham	9	Fa.	E 2		
150	PerpetuumM	Butcher	220	Pruffia	82	Stolp	12	DuNrwy	E 1			

ABBREVIATIONS.

In the Firft Column.

S,	– Ship	Sk, – Smack	Bg, – Brig	Dr, – Dogger
Sp,	– Sloop	Sr, – Schooner	G, – Galliot	Cr, – Cutter
Sw,	– Snow	St, – Schoot	H, – Hoy	K, – Ketch

s – fheathed, d – doubled, s&d – fheathed and doubled, s.C – fheathed with Copper, s.C.I.B. – fheathed with Copper and Iron Bolts, s.W.&C. – fheathed with Copper over Boards.

In Third Column.

3 Ds, Three Decks. sd, Single Deck. sdb, Single Deck with Beams. dw, Deep Waift. sdw, Single Deck with Deep Waift. Thofe Veffels, which have nothing under the Tonage, have two Decks.

In Fourth Column.

rb. rebuilt	grp. good Repair	NB. new Bottom
len. lengthened	lrp. large Repair	NUW. new Upper-
rfd, raifed	trp. thorough Repair	Works.
Drp. Damages repaired	ND. new Deck	N.Kl, new Keel.
Srprs&rp. Some Repairs	N.Sds, new Sides	

Under *the 6th Col.* L C *for Low Counter.*

The 7th Col. contains the Feet of the Draught of Water when loaded. sk. under the Draught of Water, *for Single Knees.* A, under the Owner, denotes that the Veffel is American Property.

In Eighth Column.

Surveying Ports	Be. Belfaft	Ex. Exeter	Li. Liverpool	Tn. Teingmouth
	Br. Briftol	Fa. Falmouth	Lo. London	Wa. Waterford
	Co. Cork	Gr. Greenock	Ly. Lynn	Wn Whitehaven
	Cs Cowes	Hl Hull	Mt Maryport	Wo. Workington
	Da. Dartmouth	La. Lancafter	Po. Poole	Ya. Yarmouth
	Du. Dublin	Lh Leith	Ph Portfmouth	

N. B. The abbreviated Port is always the Surveying-Port. The C. underneath the Voyage ftands for Conftant Trader. The Guns of the common Conftruction are diftinguifhed by a P. after the Number and Weight of Metal, and Carronades by a C.

The Timber, of which Veffels are built, is marked by the following Italic Letters.

B. B. Black Birch	L.O. Live Oak	S. Spruce
C. Cedar	M. Mahogany	W. H. Witch Hazel
H. Hazel	P. Pine	
J. Juniper	P. P. Pitch Pine	

The Figures from 1 to 12, under the Characters, denote the Month of the Survey in the Year 1796. Thofe Ships that have 95, 94, &c. under their Characters, have not been furveyed fince thofe Years.

The REGISTER-BOOKS *fhould be pofted every Week: and it is requefted that the Members will be particular in delivering them when they are called for, as otherwife the Office cannot be refponfible for their Correctnefs.*

Chapter two

VOYAGES

W hen the *Peggy and Isabella* was built in 1777, the American War of Independence was a year old. Being so far from the major trade route, the war would have had apparently little impact on the economic life of the Orkney Islands, and trade with the mainland would have carried on without too much interruption. The only impact the war had was the recruitment of young men into the Royal Navy. It was known that Press Gangs did operate on the Islands, but as the Navy was well aware of the quality of the seamen in these northern Islands, they would have engaged men by paying a bounty. With opportunities for employment being so low at that time, the Navy apparently found plenty of willing recruits, so that for the period of the war, there would have been a considerable shortage of young men.

In 1780, Britain was faced with a grouping of the European Nations under the Armed Neutrality Pact, which isolated her from erstwhile friendly nations. The Pact limited her trade with Russia, Sweden, Prussia and Denmark, so that Orkney's trade with the Baltic was severely curtailed. A much more serious problem was the entry of Spain and the Netherlands in 1779, and 1780, into the war on the side of the Americans. From that time, and until 1783, British ships sailing in southern coastal waters faced the very real threat of an attack from fast, well-armed French privateers.

The Orkney merchants were more concerned about developing trade with the mainland than a war on the other side of the Atlantic. Britain was enjoying a period of economic growth and the demand for raw materials was increasing. Merchants engaged in transporting kelp from Orkney, and timber and iron from the Baltic, knew that they would obtain a good return on their capital if they built and managed ships.

The demand for kelp brought considerable wealth to the Orkney Lairds which eventually resulted in a higher standard of living all round. The effect of this growth of income was that the islands, which had been self-sufficient, started to import materials and goods which had been previously unobtainable due to lack of money. One aspect of this new wealth was that coal, at one time an unheard-of luxury, was imported in large quantities and used for domestic purposes and in the production of kelp. Kelp was in demand in Newcastle and Sunderland, and, as both towns were coal producers, this meant that ships carrying a cargo of kelp would take back coal, thus enabling ship owners to make a profit even when freight rates were low.

The voyages and cargoes carried by the *Peggy and Isabella*, in the period for which records exist, are summarised below. This shows that trade with England and Scotland accounted for more than 55% of the voyages, and, of these, 64% were with a cargo on the homeward voyage. The ship was not a regular Baltic trader, with voyages taking place in 1782, 1785, 1788 and 1789, some of which were very profitable. There were, however, many ships from all British ports engaged in this trade, reducing the chance of securing a return cargo. The fact that the *Peggy and Isabella* had a reasonably high proportion of return cargoes, showed that Watt must have been an astute manager, and it was this ability to obtain them that enabled the ship to return a good profit every year. Watt would have had agents in many ports who would have secured cargoes for the ship knowing that these would be delivered timeously, in good order and at reasonable rates.

TRADING PATTERN OF THE *PEGGY AND ISABELLA*
1779, and 1782-1792

	No. of voyages	With return cargoes	Cargoes
Orkney, England, Orkney	28	18	kelp, coal
Orkney, Scotland, Orkney	14	2	kelp,coal, slate, grain, timber
Orkney, Ireland, Orkney	3	2	timber, hemp
Orkney, Norway, Orkney	3	1	bere, timber
Norway, Scotland	1	-	iron
Norway, Baltic	1	-	not known
Orkney, Sweden, Orkney	1	-	bere

Note: As Orkney was not a producer of timber and hemp, these cargoes would have been taken on board at a mainland port or delivered to Orkney by other ships. There are no entries in the disbursement records for the purchase of goods or port charges at any port other than the destination.

The specific dates on which voyages were undertaken are not given in the records, only the month in which the voyage, and the disbursement record, was completed. It is, therefore, only possible to estimate how long particular voyages lasted. Apparently the majority lasted about a month, with several lasting at least two months. Voyages were not undertaken in December (with one exception in 1785), and never in January.

The fact that the ship did not leave port in these months was no reflection on the ability of the Master. It was a realistic assessment of the practical difficulties of sailing small vessels, which were totally dependent on wind power, in the very bad weather encountered in northern waters during these months. It is a matter of record that in the 16th and 17th centuries, there was a closed season for sailing in northern waters between Martinmas (11th November), and Candlemas (2nd February). Cargoes of kelp would not have been available, and, such was the pace of life in those days, a delay of two or three months would not have affected the production of glass or alum as it would have done in a more industrialised society.

Disbursement records of other ships showed that the period when they were laid up was usually spent in carrying out repairs to the hull and rigging. There are, however, no entries for expenditure being incurred either by the crew or by tradesmen on such work during these months. It is assumed that because the *Peggy and Isabella* was a small ship which was kept in a good state of repair, that the Master and crew went back home after her last voyage, and would have carried out any maintenance when she was refloated in the following year.

The voyages made by the *Peggy and Isabella* over the period are recorded in the disbursement records, and these provide very little information other than the nature of the cargo and its rate of freight. Some firms kept letter books showing a record of transactions carried out by the manager and the Master of the ship for particular cargoes, giving an insight into the general problems that existed in obtaining and delivering cargoes.

The only letters which exist are those written by William Hewison during his voyage to Scandinavia in 1785, shown in Figures 9, 10, 11, and one written from Westray later in the year, shown in Figure 12. These first three letters provide a record of how a resourceful Master (and part-owner), faced with the prospect of returning to Kirkwall without a cargo, obtained cargoes from the Baltic and Norway, returning to Scotland with them five months later. The summary of his voyages is set out below, together with transcripts of his letters. These, however, do not record all the difficulties Hewison faced in his dealings with Norwegian merchants, port and Customs officials in Konigsberg, and in obtaining ship supplies from Norwegian and Prussian suppliers. The language spoken in Norway, Denmark and the Baltic ports was, apparently, similar in some respects to that spoken by Orcadians and people of northern Scotland. His ability to converse with people ranging from merchants, officials, suppliers and tradesmen would have made his task much easier. He would have been aided, too, by some of the many Scots who were acting as agents and merchants in their own right in the Scandinavian and Baltic ports, and who would have negotiated with local merchants, officials and suppliers and thus helped a shipmaster such as Hewison to transact business in a foreign port.

SUMMARY OF THE VOYAGES OF THE *PEGGY AND ISABELLA, 1785*

	No.of voyages		Cargo	Freight £
April /May	1	Kirkwall - Trondheim	Bere	35
May	2	Trondheim - Trondheim	Collecting cargo from wrecked ship	22
May July	3	Trondheim - Konigsburg Elsinore - Trondheim	Barley, peas	72
July Aug/	4	Trondheim - Christiansand	Sundries	7
Sept	5	Christiansand - Leith	Iron	60
Oct	1	Leith - Orkney	Sundries	17
			Total	213

The income from these Baltic voyages was lower than that obtained from trading with the mainland in previous years. Up to 1784, the ship had been very profitable, although, from 1785, the trend was towards significantly lower revenues. This may have been because of increased competition and/or lower freight rates. The possibility that cargoes would be difficult to obtain if the ship returned to Orkney, may have influenced William Hewison to stay and seek whatever was going in Norway.

HEWISON'S SCANDINAVIAN VOYAGES, 1785

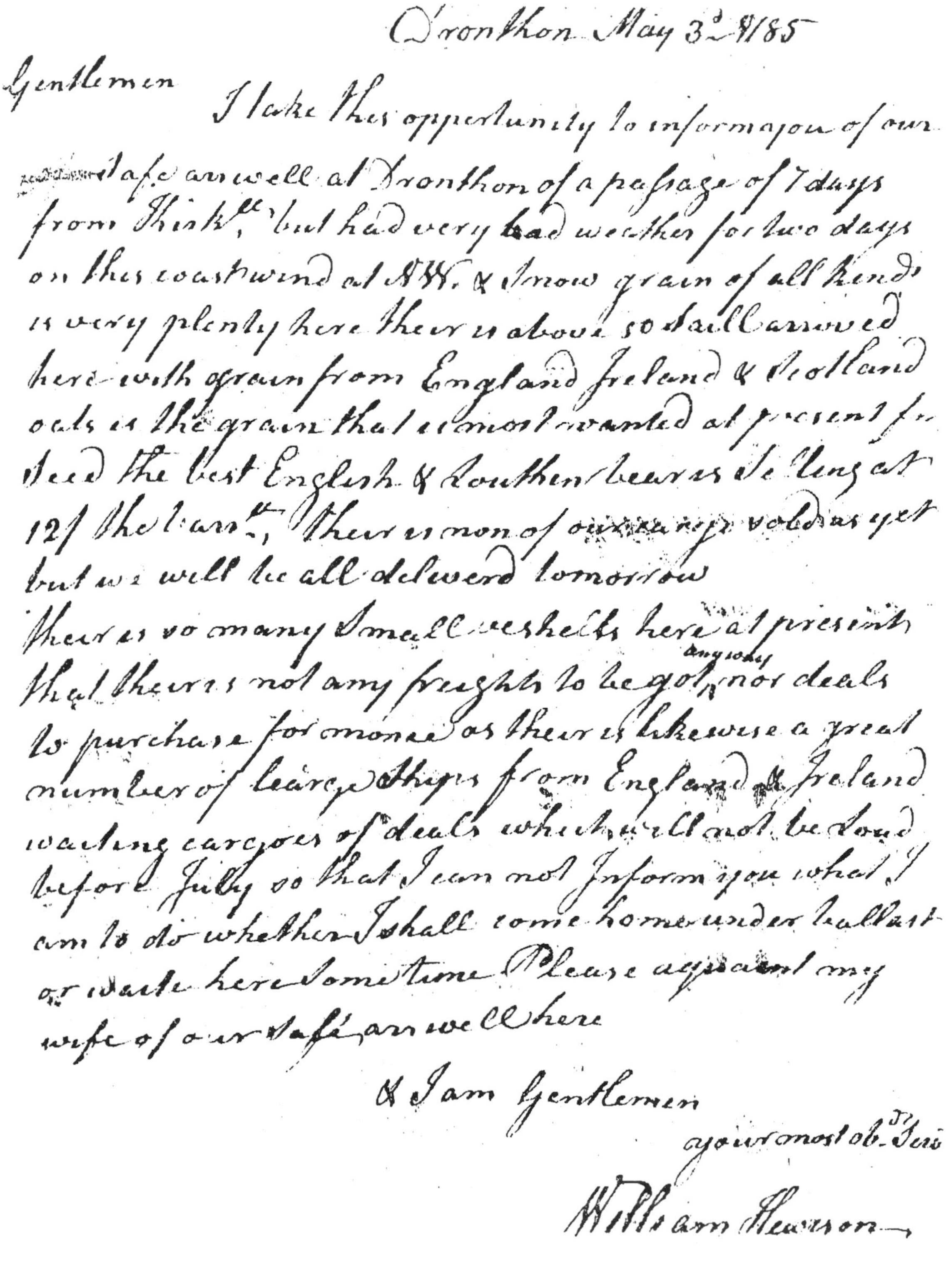

Figure 9
Letter from Hewison to Watt, May 3rd, 1785.

Figure 9, transcript:

Dronthon (1)
May 3rd 1785

I take this opportunity to inform you of our safe arrivell at Dronthon of a passage of 7 days from Kirk'll [Kirkwall], but had very bad weather for two days on this coast wind at NW & Inow [enough] grain of all kinds is very plenty here. Their is above 50 Saill arrived here with grain from England, Ireland & Scotland. Oats is the grain that is most wanted at present for Seed The best English and Southern bear (2) is Selling at 12/- the barr'll. There is non of our cargo sold (3) as yet but we will be all delivered tomorrow.

Their is so many Small veshells here at present that their is not any freights to be got any way nor deals to purchase for monie as their is likewise a great number of learge Ships from England and Ireland wanting cargoes of deals which will not be load before July so that I can not Inform you what I am to do whether I shall come home under ballast or waite here Some time. Please aquaint my wife of our Safe arrivell here.

& I am Gentlemen
your most Ob't Serv't

William Hewison

1. *Dronthon*
This was the port of Trondheim, a town on the west coast of Norway.

2. *Bear/Bere*
This was a form of barley which was grown in the Northern Islands because it ripened more easily than barley in the short growing season. Bere contained less sugar and therefore yielded less alcohol than barley, and provided the means of making liquor for countries which did not require a high quality product.

3. *Cargo*
Customs records show the cargo to be Bere.

Figure 10
Letter from Hewison to Watt, May 24, 1785.

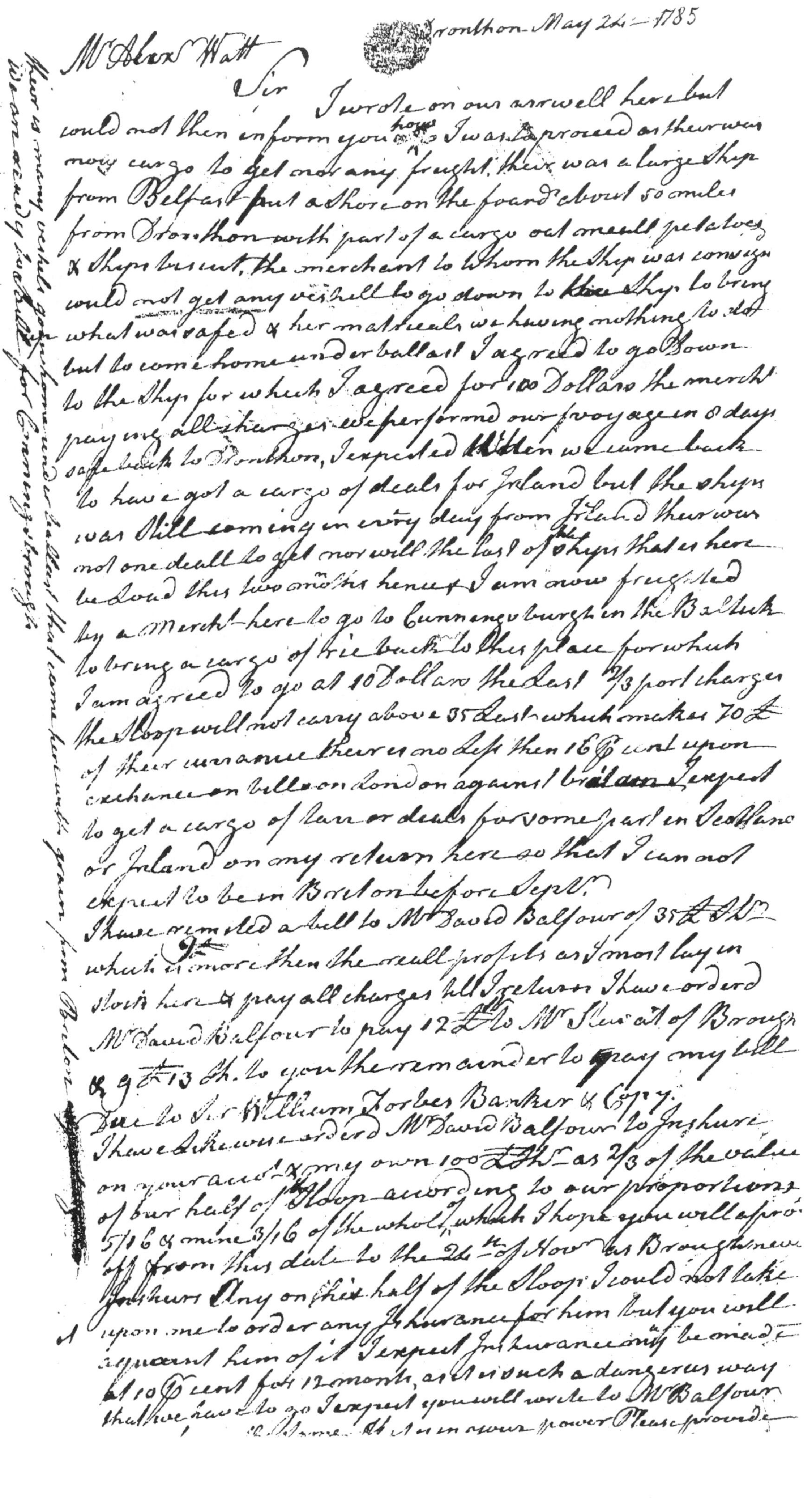

Mr Alexr Watt

Stronthon May 24 — 1785

Sir   I wrote on our arrivell here but could not then inform you how as I was to proceed as there was no cargo to get nor any fraught, their was a large ship from Belfast put ashore on the foard about 50 miles from Stronthon with part of a cargo out meall petaloes & ships bescuit, the merchant to whom the ship was consign could not get any vessell to go down to the ship to bring what was safed & her matreals, we having nothing to do but to come home under ballast I agreed to go down to the ship for which I agreed for 100 Dollars the merchts paying all charges we performd our voyage in 8 days safe back to Stronthon, I expected when we came back to have got a cargo of deals for Irland but the ships was still coming in every day from Irland their was not one deall to get nor will the last of ships that is here be loud this two months hence & I am now fraughted by a merckt here to go to Cunninesburgh in the Baltick to bring a cargo of tie back to this place for which I am agreed to go at 10 Dollars the last 2/3 port charges the sloop will not carry above 35 Last which makes 70 £ of their insurance their is no less then 16 Pr cent upon exchange on bills on London against britain I expect to get a cargo of tar or deals for some part in Scotland or Irland on my return here so that I can not expect to be in Brelton before Septr.

I have remitted a bill to Mr David Balfour of 35 £ Str which is more then the meull profits as I must lay in stock here & pay all charges till I return I have orderd Mr David Balfour to pay 12 £ to Mr Stewart of Brough & 9 £ 13 sh. to you the remainder to pay my bill due to Sir William Forbes Banker & Copy.

I have likewise orderd Mr David Balfour to Inshure on your acct & my own 100 £ Str as 2/3 of the value of our half of Sloop according to our proportions 5/16 & mine 3/16 of the whole, which I hope you will aproo off from this date to the 24th of Novr as Broughneu fathers Any on this half of the Sloop I could not take upon me to order any Inshurance for him but you will aquant him of it I expect Inshurance only be made at £ 10 Pr cent for 12 months, as it is such a dangerous way that we have to go I expect you will write to Mr Balfour & Stewart As soon as in our power Please provide

(margin, vertical text):
Me a vessel of some kind with grain from Brelton We are now by too bills [...] for Grennig & through us an early [...]

Figure 10, transcript:

Dronthon May 24th 1785

Mr Alexr Watt
Sir
*I wrote on our arrivell here but could not then inform you how I was to proceed as their
was no[?] cargo to get nor any freight. There was a large Ship from Belfast put ashore
on the foard about 50 miles from Dronthon with part of a cargo oat meall, potatoes &
Ships biscuit. The merchant to Whom the Ship was consigned could not get any veshell
to go down to the Ship to bring what was safe & her matereals we having nothing to do
but to come home under ballast I agreed to go down to the Ship for which I agreed for
100 Dollars (1) the merch't paying all charges. We performed our voyage in 8 days
safe back to Dronthon, I expected when we came back to have got a cargo of deals for
Ireland but the ships was still coming in every day from Ireland their was not one deall
to get not will the last of the ships that is here be load this two months hence & I am
now freighted by a merchant here to go to Cunningsburgh (2) in the Baltick to bring a
cargo of ric (3) back to this place for which I am agreed to go at 10 dollars the Last (4)
2/3 port charges (5). The Sloop will not carry above 35 Lasts which makes 70£ of their
insurance their is no less than 16 [per] cent upon exchange on bills on [ ] against [ ].
I expect to get a cargo of tarr or deals for some port in Scotland or Ireland on my
return here so that I can not expect to be in Briton before Septr.
I have remited a bill to Mr David Balfour (6) of 35£ Sh[?] which is more than the reall
profits as I must lay in stock here & pay all charges till I return. I have ordered Mr
David Balfour to pay 12£[] to Mr Stewart of Brough (7) &9£ 13 Sh. to you the remainder to pay my bill due to Sir William Forbes Banker & Copy[company].
I have likewise ordered Mr David Balfour to inshure on your acc't and my own 100£
Sh- as 2/3 of the value of our half of the Sloop according to our proportions $^5/_{16}$ of mine
$^3/_{16}$ of the whole of which I hope you will apro [approve] off from this date to the 24th of
Novr as Brough never inshurs Any on their half of the Sloop I could not take it upon me
to order any Inshurance for him but you will aquaint him of it I expect Inshurance may
be made at 10 per cent for 12 months, as it is such a dangerous way that we have to go
I expect you will write to Mr Balfour [ ] if it is in your power Please provide
(their is many veshells going home under ballast that came here with grain from Briton.
We are ready to Sail for Cunningsbrough (2)).*

1. Norwegian Currency was in Rix Bank Dollars: 5 dollars = £1

2. *Cunningsburgh:* Konigsberg.

3. Ric
It is assumed the cargo was rice.

4. *Last*
A measure equivalent to 2 tons.

5. *Two third port charges*
It was the practice for merchants to pay all or part of these charges.

6. *Mr David Balfour*
The lawyer in Edinburgh who acted for William Watt.

7. *Mr Stewart of Brugh*
Half owner of the *Peggy and Isabella*. It appears that Capt Hewison and Mr Stewart
were not always in agreement, and Mr Watt was used as intermediary.

Figure 11
Letter from Hewison to Watt, July 7, 1785.

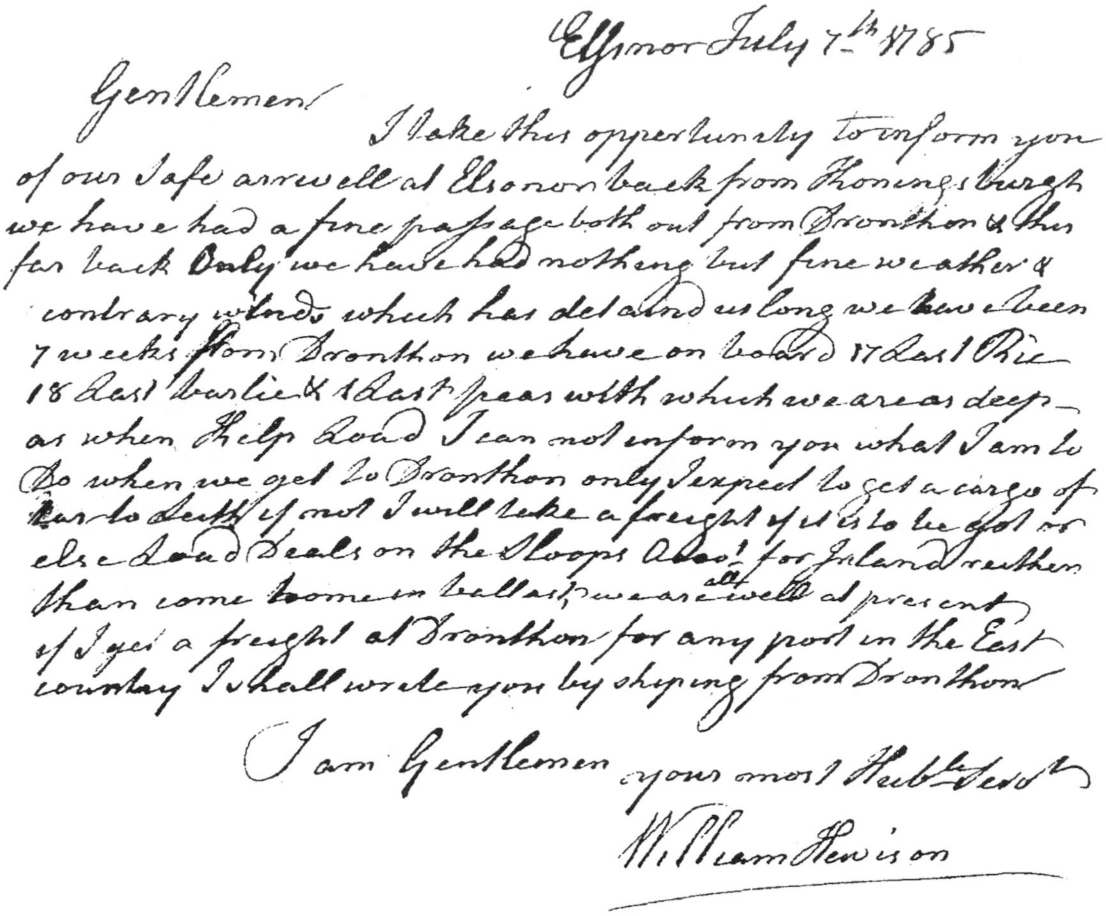

Elsinor July 7th 1785

Gentlemen

I take this opperlunity to inform you of our safe arrivell at Elsonor back from Koningsburgh we have had a fine passage both out from Dronthon & this far back Only we have had nothing but fine weather & contrary winds which has detaind us long we have been 7 weeks from Dronthon we have on board 17 Last Ric 18 Last barlie & 1 Last peas with which we are as deep as when Kelp Load I can not inform you what I am to do when we get to Dronthon only I expect to get a cargo of tar to Leith if not I will take a freight if it is to be got or else Load Deals on the Sloops Also for Ireland rather than come home in ballast we are all well at present if I get a freight at Dronthon for any port in the East country I shall write you by shiping from Dronthon

I am Gentlemen your most Hub.le Serv.t

William Hewison

Figure 11, transcript:

Elsinor (1) *July 7th 1785*

Gentlemen

I take this opportunity to inform you of our safe arrivell at Elsinor back from Konings-burgh (2) *We have had a fine passage both out from Dronthon & this far back Only we have had nothing but fine weather & contrary winds which has detaind us long we have been 7 weeks from Dronthon we have on board 17 Last Ric*[rice] *18 Last barlie and 1 Last peas with which we are as deep as when Kelp Load. I can not inform you what I am to do when we get to Dronthon only I expect to get a cargo of tar[?] to Leath if not I will take a freight if it is to be got or else load deals on the Sloops Also [] for Ireland rather than come in ballast We are all well at present if I get a freight at Dronthon for any port in the East country I shall write you by shiping from Dronthon.*

I am Gentlemen your Most Hub'le Serv't

William Hewison

1. The Danish Government levied a tax on all ships (entering or leaving the Baltic), that passed through the Straits between Denmark and Sweden. Ships anchored at Elsinore and awaited inspection by Customs officials before paying dues.

2. *Koningsburgh*
Konigsberg.

THE DUMBARTON VOYAGE

Captain Hewison, on his return from Leith in October, obviously considered he had completed an arduous season of trading, and, by the end of the month it was time to haul the *Peggy and Isabella* onto the beach. Mr Stewart, however, had been offered the chance to sail a cargo of kelp to Dumbarton and had instructed Hewsison to deliver the cargo. Hewison was accustomed to receiving his instructions for transporting cargoes from William Watt, and thus wrote to him to ascertain if he agreed with the proposed venture. According to the disbursement records, the voyage to Dumbarton and back to Orkney was completed by the end of December. The weather in northern waters was usually very bad in November/December, and the voyage would not have been undertaken without some risk to ship and crew.

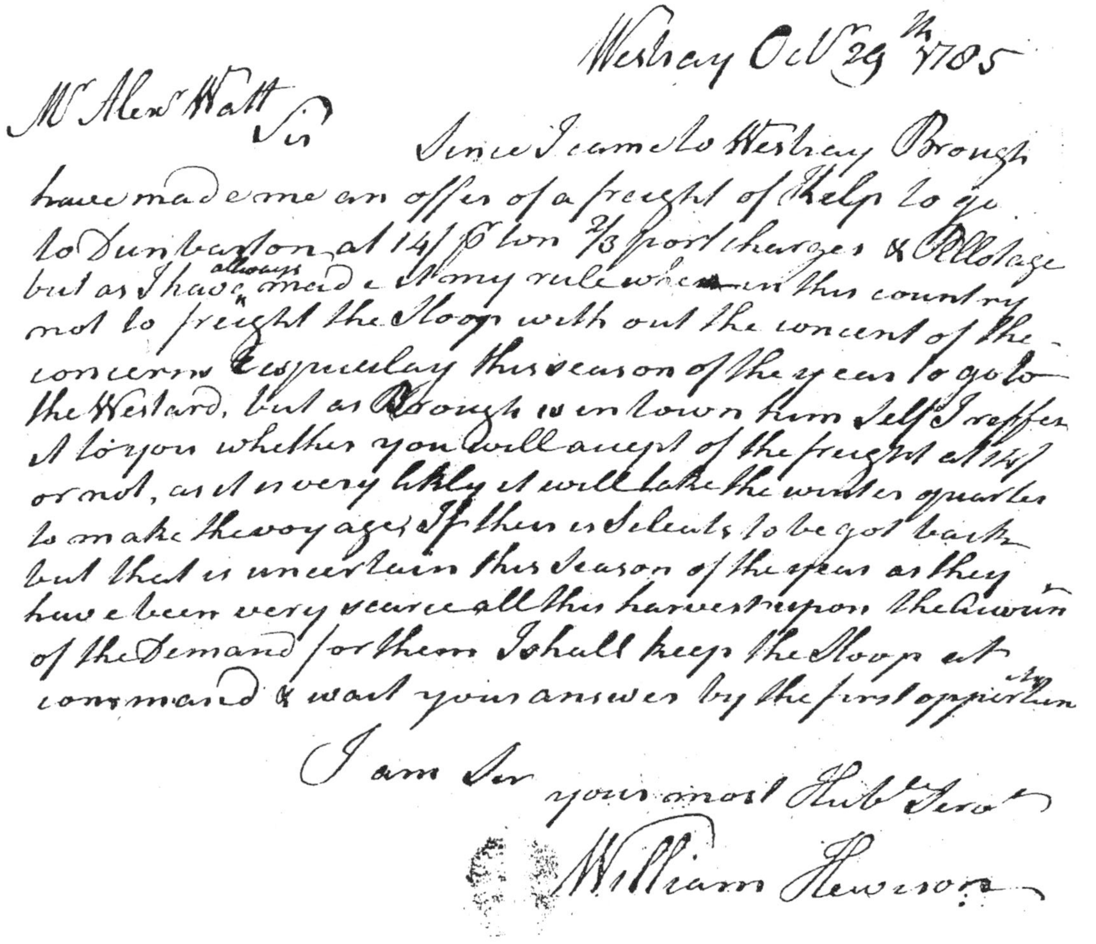

Figure 12
Letter from Hewison to Watt, Oct. 29, 1785.

Figure 12, transcript:

Westray
Oct 29th 1785

Mr Aleẋr Watt

Sir
Since I came to Westray Brough(1) have made me an offer of a freight of Kelp to go to Dumbarton at 14/- per ton 2/3 port charges & pillotage but as I have always made it my rule when in this country not to freight the Sloop with out the consent of concernd Especulay this season of the year to go to the Westard, but as Brough is in the town him Self I reffer it to you whether you will accept of the freight at 14/- or not, as it very

37

likly it will take the winter quarter to make the voyage If their is scleats (2) to be got back but that is uncertain this Season of the year as they have been very scarce all this harvest upon the account of the demand for them. I shall keep the Sloop at command & wait your answer by the first opportunity.

I am Sir

your most Hub'le Serv't

William Hewison

1. *Brough*
James Stewart, Laird of Brugh.

2. *Scleats:* Slates

It is obvious that Captain Hewison was not willing to undertake a voyage to the West Coast as the voyage would take until the end of the year, and it was doubtful if a return cargo of slates would be obtained. The disbursement records for the period, however, recording income from the freight of kelp to Dumbarton, show that Mr Watt obviously did not share his view that such a venture would not be remunerative, thus William Hewison and the *Peggy and Isabella* had one last voyage before they finished a busy year.

RECORD OF VOYAGES OF THE *SKIRMISH*

The only source of information on the time taken by ships of this period on voyages to certain ports, and on the engagement of crew, is the record of voyages undertaken by the sloop *Skirmish* from 1st May, 1792, to 2nd February, 1793, which are contained in the Balfour Papers. She would not have been a very profitable ship as her cargo carrying capacity was low, and the cost of operating the ship set against the freight income would have been high. The *Peggy and Isabella*'s operating costs would not have been that much greater yet her earning potential was much higher. No doubt it was for this reason that William Watt and his partners purchased a larger vessel.

The *Skirmish* records were not as well maintained as those of the *Peggy and Isabella*, and there is no record of income and expenditure, apart from the freight paid for a cargo in May, and the monthly wage rates of the Master and crew. The rate paid to the Master, 30/- per month, was not high, and it can be assumed that the *Skirmish* was a small ship between 40-50 tons. The record of her voyages, given in Figure 13, is not always legible, but interesting in that it shows that the ship sometimes sailed considerable distances, and the time taken on those voyages.

The records of the *Peggy and Isabella* provide a considerable amount of information on expenditure incurred on the ship and her crew, but they do not give the dates on which voyages commenced and finished, and they do not show when members of the crew were appointed and discharged.

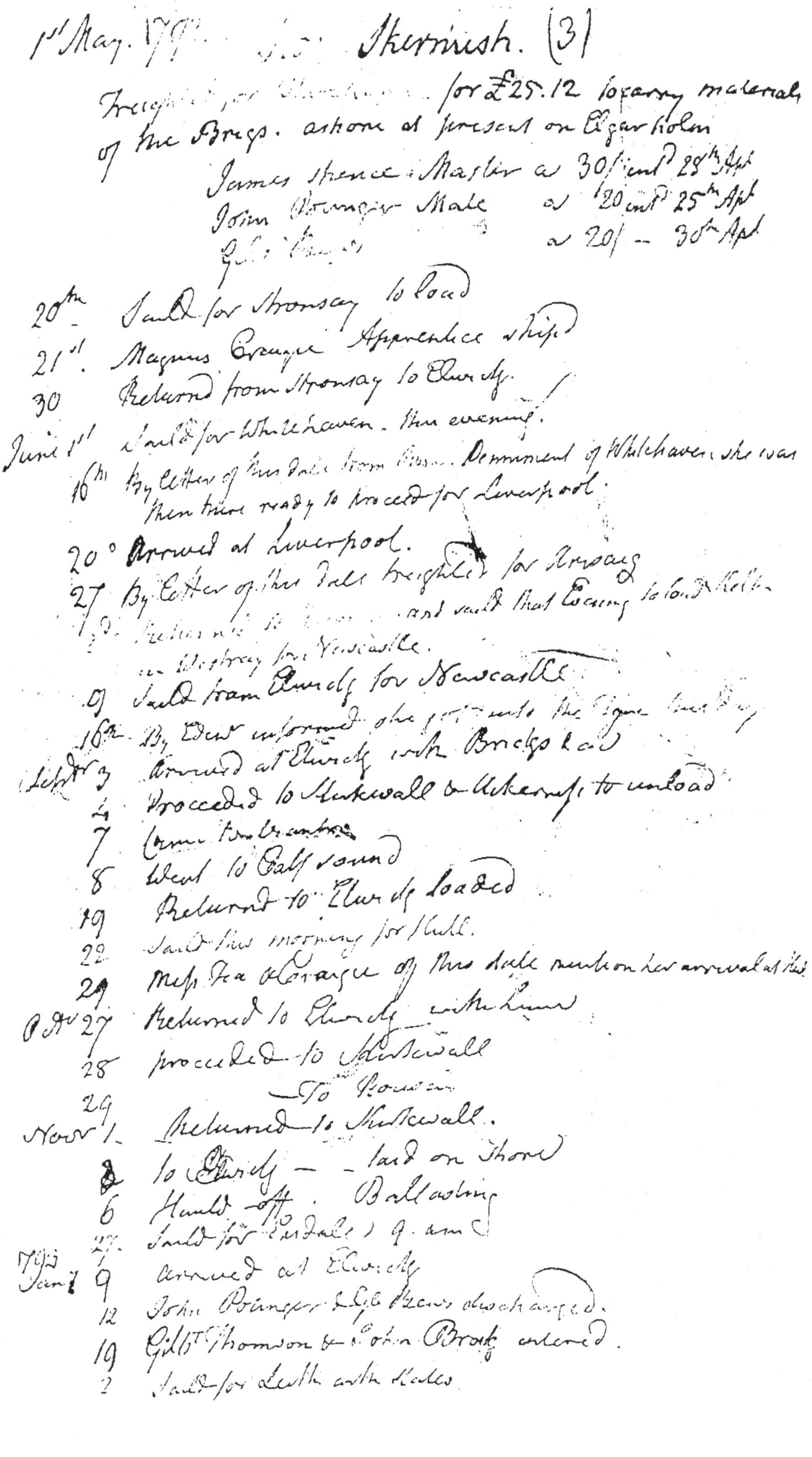

1st May. 179[?]   [?]: Skirmish. (3)

Figure 13
Record of
voyages of
the *Skirmish*,
1792-3.

Freigh[?] [?] [?]...... for £25.12 to carry materials
of the Brigs. ashore at present on Elgar holen

    James Spence Master a 30/ [?] 28th Apl
    John [?]inger Mate   a 20 [?] 25th Apl
    G[?] [?]   a 20/ — 30th Apl

20th   Sail'd for Stronsay to load
21st   Magnus Erauge Apprentice ship'd
30   Return'd from Stronsay to Elwick.
June 1st   Sail'd for Whitehaven. this evening.
16th   By Letter of this date from [?]. Detenment of Whitehaven, she was
     then there ready to proceed for Liverpool.
20°   Arrived at Liverpool.
27   By Letter of this date freight'd for [?]
     [?] and sail'd that Evening to [?]
     [?] for Newcastle.
....   Sail'd from [?] for Newcastle
16th   By [?] inform'd she [?]
[?]3   Arrived at Elwick with Bricks load
4   Proceeded to Kirkwall & [?] to unload
7   Came [?]
8   Went to Calf sound
19   Return'd to Elwick loaded
22   Sail'd this morning for Hull.
29   Mess[?] [?] & Erauge of this date [?] on her arrival at this
Oct 27   Return'd to Elwick with Lime
28   proceeded to Kirkwall
     —To [?]
29
Novr 1.   Return'd to Kirkwall.
2   to Elwick — — laid on Shore
6   Hauld off. Ballasting
27   Sail'd for [?] 9 am
[?]
Jan 9   Arrived at Elwick
12   John [?]inger & [?] crews discharged.
19   Gilbt Thomson & John Brok enter'd.
2   Sail'd for Leith with [?]

Figure 13, transcript:

1st May, 1792. sloop Skirmish.

 Freight. for */or £25.12 to carry materials*
 of the Brigs.[Hellier Holm] *ashore at present on Elgarholm*
  James Spence Master @ 30/- 28th April
  John Potinger Mate @ 20/- 25th April
  Gib Bews @ 20/- 30th April

20	*Saild for Stronsay to load*
21	*Magnus Craigie Apprentice ship'd*
30	*Returned from Stronsay to Elwick*
June 1	*Sail'd for Whitehaven this evening.* [with kelp]
16	*By letter of this date from Mrs Drummond of Whitehaven, she was then [ ] ready to proceed for Liverpool.*
20	*Arrived at Liverpool.*
27	*By letter of this date freighted for Arisaig* [cargo, grain].
?July 2	*Returned to Elwick and saild that Evening to load kelp on Westray for Newcastle.*
9	*Saild from Elwick for Newcastle*
16	*By Edin. informed she got into the Tyne*[?] *this day*
Sept 3	*Arrived at Elwick with Bricks Load*[?]
4	*Proceeded to Kirkwall & Aikerness*[?] *to unload*
7	*Came to [ ]*
8	*Went to Calf Sound*
19	*Returned to Elwick loaded*
22	*Saild this morning for Hull*
29	*Mess. Fea [ ] of this date mention her arrival at Hull*
Oct 27	*Returned to Elwick with hemp*[?]
28	*Proceeded to Kirkwall*
29	*[Proceeded] to [Rousay?]*
Nov 1	*Returned to Kirkwall.*
3	*To Elwick - laid on shore*
6	*Hauld off. Ballasting*
27	*Saild for Easdale 9am*
1793 Jan 9	*Arrived at Elwick*
12	*John Pottinger & Gib Bews discharged.*
19	*Gilbt Thomson & John Brass entered.*
Feb 2	*Sail'd for Leith with slates*

The record of her voyages can be summarised as follows:

May	Unloading cargo at Elgarholm	
June	Whitehaven	Kelp
	Whitehaven to Liverpool	Not stated
	Liverpool to Arisaig	Grain?
July	Elwick to Newcastle	Kelp
Aug/Sept	Newcastle, Elwick	Bricks
Sept	Elwick, Hull	Kelp
Oct.	Hull, Elwick	Not clear
Nov.	Laid up, ballasted	
?Nov.	Elwick, Easdale	Ballast
Jan.	Easdale, Elwick	Slates
Feb.	Elwick, Leith	Slates

Chapter three

KELP, COAL AND SLATE

B ecause of the benefit the income from kelp brought to Orkney, there are many comments about it in the *Old Statistical Account*. The most complete statement on the collection and manufacture of kelp is given by the minister of the Parish of Shapinsay in the *Old Statistical Account* (1780), reproduced in Appendix II. The islands benefited from a period of sustained growth which continued until 1830, and all sections of the community improved their standard of living.

The production of kelp in the 18th century was a crude process*. Seaweed was burnt in circular pits five feet in diameter, and a foot deep, with a sand or earth floor. The fuel in those days was peat, driftwood, and, latterly, coal, and the whole process took two days. The seaweed turned initially into a liquid, and then solidified into a hard mass. This had to be broken into lumps which were taken by cart to stores from where they were loaded onto ships.

The base of this solid lump of kelp was composed of sand, earth and stones, which was of little use to the glass producers. The lairds made little or no effort to improve their methods in order to reduce the amount of these impurities and instead made allowance for waste by supplying kelp at a tonnage rate of 21cwts. As a result of further complaints from the glass producers it was agreed to increase the tonnage rate to 22cwts.

A product which was comprised of large and small pieces would have been difficult to transport from the store to a ship. Apparently, it was taken in sacks or creels on the backs of men and women and dumped into the hold of the ship. This was the most suitable method of loading it, as the cargo could be distributed evenly and would be less likely to shift during the voyage than a loose cargo.

The development of markets for kelp took many years. Between 1740 and 1760, the price per ton was 45/-, and, from 1760 to 1770, it was £4.4/-. Demand then markedly increased (because of the Industrial Revolution), and the price rose between 1770 and 1790, to between £5-£6 per ton. (The kelp was used in the manufacture of glass, soap and alum and the bleaching of cloth.) The ports which were the major kelp importers were Leith, Newcastle and Sunderland.

*The collection, manufacture and marketing of kelp in the 18th and 19th centuries, has been very well set out in *Kelp Making in Orkney*, by WLP Thomson.

The freight rates for transporting kelp in 1776, when the decision was made to purchase a new ship, are not available. From the limited records available, however, it is possible to estimate that they were high enough to make the transportation a profitable one. The rates per ton from 1789 to 1792, are set out below.

Year	Rates Obtained	Weight of Cargo	Revenue
1779	15/- 17/-	77 t 5 cwt	£57. 18 9
1782	16/-	74 t 16 cwt	£59. 11 -
1783	14/- 10/-	73 t 6 cwt	£38. 11 -
1786/92	14/- 12/- 10/-	75 t 15 cwt	£37. 17

The demand for kelp remained stable throughout the period, and the only explanation for the fall in rates, from 1783 onwards, was the end of the American War of Independence in 1783. Many local men served in the Navy during the war, which was as quick to release men at the end of hostilities as it was to recruit them at the beginning. Thus, there would have been a large number of trained seamen available for employment from 1783. No doubt ships had been laid up due to lack of men, and with crews available again, there would have been plenty of competition for cargoes.

It is on record that there were 30 ships engaged in transporting kelp at this time. The reduction in the freight rates would not have affected William Watt too much, as his firm were also coal merchants and would have offset the loss of revenue from kelp by the freight and sale of coal.

The rates for carrying coal varied considerably over the period, as the following table shows:-

1782 - 1787	25/- - 15/- per ton
1787 - 1792	5/8 - 6/- per ton

There is no apparent reason why rates fell in 1787. The English coal owners, and latterly their counterparts in Scotland, had increased production in order to meet rising industrial and commercial demand. There was a large number of small ships engaged in the transportation of coal round the British Isles and the sheer availability of shipping, not necessarily owned by local shipowners, may have been the reason for bringing down prices.

Coal was a relatively easy commodity to tax, and for a long period had been subject to heavy and discriminatory taxation. Early in the 18th Century, a tax of 3/8d per ton, was imposed on all coal carried by coastal shipping, and this tax was increased in 1779, 1782 and 1787. The Reverend George Barry, who wrote the entry in the *Old Statistical Account for Kirkwall and St Ola* in 1780, considered the tax to be "unjust and impolitic". It would seem that he was not the only person in Orkney to hold this view. Indeed, it was considered to be a very unfair tax throughout the country.

The Customs Register for Orkney for the period 1782-1792, records the duty paid on cargoes of coal coming into Kirkwall, and it is noteworthy that the number of recorded cargoes is considerably less than the number of cargoes of coal entered in the disbursement records of the *Peggy and Isabella*. In the period 1782 -1792, 16 cargoes of coal were carried to Orkney and duty was paid on only five occasions.

Mr Watt had plenty of experience evading Customs duties on liquor and tobacco in the 1760's and 1770's, when this was a generally accepted practice amongst local merchants. By the 1780's, however, it was not condoned and Watt apparently paid duty on whisky, brandy and tobacco like everyone else. (At least, no record exists of action taken by Customs Officials against him during the 1780's.) Another incentive to stop evasion may have been that Excise men were more effective and penalties more onerous. The evasion of coal duty, however, did not have the same social stigma and the *Peggy and Isabella* would have been able to off-load her cargoes on outlying beaches without fear of being reported to the Excise men. It is not surprising that Watt evaded the coal tax, as he paid £6.11.4 for just one cargo of coal in 1782.

The rates quoted for coal in the records are based on different measures during the period; per keel (21 tons 4cwt), chaldron (2 tons 13cwt), boll (6cwt) and barrels (1 1/2-2cwt). The measures for keels, chaldrons, bolls and barrels varied in different parts of the country and the figures quoted are an average of these different rates.

The only other cargo where it is possible to compare rates over a period is slate. Rates for carrying it did not vary significantly; 36/- per thousand in 1783 and 33/- per thousand in 1792.

CARGO HANDLING

It is on record that kelp was loaded on to the ships by means of large baskets. Whether the kelp was stored in the hold in these baskets is not known. It is likely that it was stored loose in the hold, as the majority of the cargo was in large lumps which would not have shifted very much in the hold in bad weather.

Cargoes of coal may have been loaded in sacks, as it was comprised of relatively small pieces. The use of sacks would have made it much easier to handle the coal, and they could have been easily stacked in the hold to form a stable cargo. It is unlikely, however, that the consignors would have purchased sacks, and coal was probably loaded and unloaded using baskets. Labour was cheap in those days.

The ship frequently carried kelp and coal consecutively for several voyages and the fact that each cargo would contain dust from the other, would not have mattered too much to the consignors.

Grain, being a foodstuff, would have been less valuable if contaminated with kelp and coal dust, and it required a different treatment when being moved by sea. It is likely, because of its nature, that it was carried in sacks which would have made handling easier. It was the practice in earlier times to carry grain in bulk, and the hold was lined with planks in order to avoid the cargo getting in to the bilges.

Slates, being heavy and liable to being broken, would have been carried in pallets and may have been the easiest cargo to be transported.

Regardless of the nature of the cargo, the actual task of moving the goods on or off the ship would have involved a lot of very hard work by the crew. The actual handling of "dirty" cargoes, such as kelp and coal, in the confined space of the hold would have been particularly unpleasant. It was very important that cargoes were stored correctly to avoid straining the hull, and that they were stored in such a manner that the vessel was not too low at the stern or at the bow. Some shipmasters found that their ship sailed better when it was very slightly lower at the stern and would make minor adjustments to the distribution of the cargo to bring this about. It was also very important to store cargoes so that they did not shift when the ship was under sail. To avoid this happening with loose cargoes, wooden partitions were put in the hold.

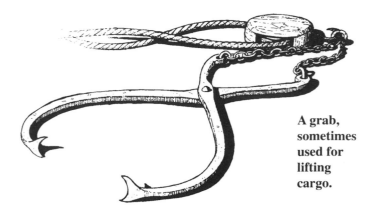

A grab, sometimes used for lifting cargo.

Cargoes were not lifted manually from the hold to the deck and then to the quay, or to a cart. Loose kelp and coal were loaded into baskets and lifted by a rope which went through a block or pulley attached to the mast by a strong iron bracket. These blocks were specially made for the purpose, as they had a large hook at one end for attachment to the mast bracket. If the ship was on dry land, and tilted to one side, it was an easy matter for the load to be swung over the side and into the cart. When the ship was at a quayside, the baskets had to be carried across a gangway to the shore by members of the crew. It was also possible for spurs to be fitted to hoops at the lower end of the mast which enabled cargoes to be moved from the deck to the quay or cart.

The sloop was only capable of taking cargoes which could be moved from and to the hold in relatively small quantities. It could not lift heavy items such as large barrels of wine, which could weigh up to a ton. The *Peggy and Isabella*, however, was effective in the handling of bulk cargoes which on average weighed between 50-70 tons.

Unloading cargo from a beached sloop.

Chapter four

NAVIGATION

Masters of vessels employed in the Coastal and Baltic trade in the 18th century, had at their disposal very basic means for navigating the vessel from one port to another. The safe passage of ships depended largely on the experience of the Master who would have served a considerable time at sea and proved himself to be a competent navigator before being given command of a ship. Navigating in those days was more a hard-earned skill than a science and there were considerable losses amongst the small coasting vessels. The fact that the *Peggy and Isabella* survived for 30 years was proof that her Masters were skilled in this art.

The navigational aids which would have been employed on the *Peggy and Isabella* are discussed in this chapter.

Compass

A compass as a means of determining direction has been used for many centuries by mariners. It was situated in port of the helmsman and mounted in gimbals, which were brass rings enabling the compass to remain level. It was kept in a box called a binnacle, which also contained a lamp which was situated at the back of the compass to illuminate it. These early instruments were inaccurate and subject to considerable variation, but by the end of the 18th century they were much more reliable.

The compass which would have been in use on the *Peggy and Isabella* would have consisted of a card marked with 32 points, with a needle mounted so that it turned freely, housed in a brass case and protected by glass. There was also a "tell tale" compass kept by the Master's bunk so that he could check the direction in which the ship was travelling.

It was not an easy task for a helmsman to steer a sailing ship along a given course because the constant movement of a small vessel meant that the compass card and needle were continually in motion. Not all helmsmen had the necessary experience in order to steer a ship, and Masters would be constantly checking the direction by means of the tell tale compass when they were not on deck.

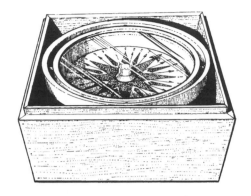

A wooden, boxed compass.

There were various spellings used over the centuries for the housing of the compass. These ranged from *Betakle* in the 15th century, *Bitakell* in the 16th century, to *Binacle* in the 18th century. William Hewison used the term *Banacle*, which differs from the spelling used in certain maritime records, but is clearly for the housing of a compass.

Lead line

This was a weight attached to a line and used to determine the depth of water beneath a ship. The normal line length for vessels employed on coastal work was 20 fathoms, and there was a distinguishing mark at every fathom. The majority of the voyages undertaken by the *Peggy and Isabella* were in the shallow waters of the Scottish and English coasts, and these waters were subject to a rapid rise and fall of the tides twice daily. An experienced Master would have a record of the tides along his regular routes

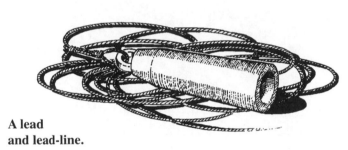

A lead and lead-line.

and the nature of the seabed. When approaching a coast at night, or at a time of poor visibility, tallow would be put on the weight so that it was possible to check both the depth of the water and the nature of the seabed. These soundings would be taken frequently, and, given the Master's knowledge of the depth of water round various anchorages, would provide him with a reasonable indication of his position.

Log

The log, and log-line, was an English invention of the 16th century, used to measure the distance sailed by a ship in a given time and thence to estimate the distance sailed over a longer period of time. The log used by William Hewison would have consisted of a line knotted at regular intervals, with a float at one end which was wound on a reel placed on the stern of the ship. To determine the number of knots which the ship was

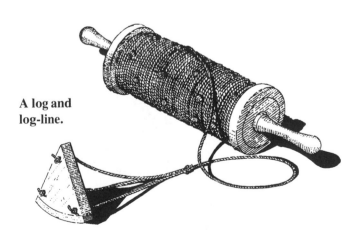

A log and log-line.

travelling, the float was thrown over the side and the number of knots passing over the stern over a given time (usually recorded by a small sand glass), was recorded.

An inventory of the sails and equipment of the sloop *Good Intent*, made in 1790, (given in Appendix I), lists the following items: A lead line; wooden boxed compasses; sand glasses, (2 hours, 1 hour, 1/2 hour); a compass in the cabin.

The only item missing is the log for measuring speed, which is surprising as the three different sizes of hourglass were used in conjunction with the log.

Sailing Directions

An accurate chart for the northern coast of Scotland was not published until 1792, and this was probably not generally available in Orkney. Masters such as Hewison, would be dependent upon Sailing Directions, which gave the course to be steered, the overall distance between ports, distances between landmarks, details of tides and currents and any other relevant information. Directions such as these, called *Rutters*, had been used by mariners since medieval times and the earliest known example for Scotland was called a *Rutter of the Northern Seas* by Alexander Lindsay, dated 1540. The term *Rutter*, was derived from the French term *Routier*. These Sailing Directions were the forerunners of the present day *North Sea Pilot* and are very accurate, considering the basic navigational instruments available in the 16th century. Some of Lindsay's Sailing Directions for Leith and the east coast of Scotland are reproduced in Figure 14.

Figure 14
**Sailing
Directions,
1540.**

Sixteenth Century Navigation
Leith and the East Coast of Scotland

Compiled from information supplied by Alexander Lindsay
Pilot to James V, 1540

<u>Leith and the Forth</u>

Tides

At Leith, when it blows, the tides run SSW and NNE.
From Leith to St Abbs Head, when the moon is S by W it is full sea.
From the Road of Leith to the Isle of May the tide runs SSW and NNE.

Courses

1 Heading South
In sailing to the north between Leith and Kinghorn, the South course to the
Bass must be N by E and S by W.
From the Bass to St Abbs Head, the course is ESE and WNW.

2 Heading North
From the Road of Leith to Inchkeith, NNE.
From Inchkeith to the May or the Point of Fife, NE by E.
The May and the Point of Fife lie S and N.

Soundings

If you would stay in the Road of Leith, cast anchor at NW or WNW straight against the town of Leith, and you shall have 7 fathoms of water at full sea and 3 1/2 at low water.

Distances

Leith to St Abbs head - 60 miles   *Leith to Inchkeith - 4 miles*
Inchkeith to the May - 20 miles   *The May to Fifeness - 8 miles*
Inchkeith to Fifeness - 28 miles

Fifeness to Aberdeen

Tides

From the point of Fife to the point called Red Head, along the coast of Aberdeen to Buchanness, the tides run SSW and NNE.

Courses

The Point of Fife and Red head lie S by W and N by E.
The Point of Fife to St Andrews, W by N.
The Point of Fife to the mouth of the Tay, N by W.
Red Head and Montrose lie S and N.
The coasts of Aberdeen, Buchanness and Torrishness lie SSE and NNW.

Soundings

If you would put in at St Andrews, cast anchor a mile from the town, where you shall find a good bottom and 7 fathoms of water.

Dangers

If you would pass Fifeness, you must notice a danger called Carwick, which lies ENE from the coast. The best way to avoid it is to have the steeple of Crail in your view.

If you would enter Dundee, keep the north side of the church upon the bar, and on the NW straight over against Broughty, because there is a dangerous sand called Brumlaw.

Between Fifeness and Red Head, 12 miles SE of Red Head, there lies a danger called Inchcop.

If you would enter the haven of Montrose, hold to the south side of that entry, so you shall shun a bank of sand.

On the coast of Aberdeen, not far from the shore, lies a rock called the Girdill. If you would enter the harbour, take threequarters of the tide with you, because there lies a dangerous bank of sand in the mouth of the river.

Distances

Fifeness to the mouth of the Tay - 11 miles   Point of Fife to Red Head - 19 miles
Red Head to the coast of Aberdeen - 33 miles

William Hewison would have been able to use the modern equivalent of Sailing Directions in his voyages from Orkney to Leith and Newcastle, as many of the land-marks he used are still there. He might be puzzled by some of the structures constructed in the 19th and 20th centuries, such as the Forth-Tay Bridges and lighthouses. By and large, however, most of the information would be relevant still.

A set of Sailing Directions, taken from Murdo McKenzie's *General Chart of the East Coast of Scotland*, 1792, is given below.

Observation

"From the Naye of Norway to Duncansby Head or Pentland Firth being the passage between Scotland and the Orkneys into the Atlantic Ocean, the course is NW by W westerly 125 Leagues - on entering the Firth leave the Skerries to the northward and steer NNW 1/2W 5 or 6 miles for the north end of Stroma which leave to the southward. Great regard should be paid to the velocity of the tides which in Spring run 9 knots and in Neaps 3 or 4. The islands Swona and Stroma are nearly one league distant and have strong eddies under the east side of them upon a flood and on the contrary side on the ebb. If the wind is foul or not eneough to stem the tide you may anchor on the east side of Stroma by working in the eddy. The course between Stroma and Swona is a fair way between Duncansby Head on the East Coast of Scotland and -ness in the Orkneys is WNN or WNN 1/2 W 8 miles which will bring you to the west entrance of the Firth from thence a WNN 1/2 N or NW by W course will run you between Cape Wrath and the Stack Skerries they Bearing NE by E from Cape Wrath 9 leagues."

William Hewison, who, by the time he became Master of the *Peggy and Isabella* at the age of 33, would have been at sea for some 20 years and would have put together his own set of Sailing Directions, from his own knowledge of routes and the experience of other Masters. These would have been good enough for sailing between Orkney and any of the ports on the Mainland, for he could check his position from well-known landmarks.

It would be a different matter when he had to undertake a voyage to the Baltic, for he would be out of sight of land for possibly three days. As an experienced Master, however, Hewison would have been able to set and steer a course. He knew of the effect of leeway (the divergence ships can take from the proposed direction because of the effects of wind and tide, or the result of bad steering), and he would be experienced in the use of the log.

Using these methods and instruments, and given good weather with steady winds, an experienced Master would find it easy to reckon how far his vessel had sailed in 24 hours. The conditions were rarely ideal, however, and a Master would have to be experienced enough to work out his position, taking into account direction, speed of the vessel and the effect of the wind. He would have noted wind direction throughout the voyage, and checked his speed perhaps several times during the day, so it was far from simple guesswork.

The best proof of the effectiveness of basic navigational instruments is the fact that William Hewison was Master of the *Peggy and Isabella* and the *Pomona* for 20 years, and sailed to many ports in Britain, the Baltic and the Low Countries without causing harm to either of these vessels.

Traverse board

The traverse board was a simple and effective method enabling a Master to determine his position at the end of any given time. It was a round board marked with the points of the compass, with holes along the lines from the centre to each point. Using a half-hour sand glass, the helmsman marked the direction travelled in the previous half-hour by inserting a peg on the compass course. A Master could then determine the ship's general direction over a defined period of time, and, together with the speed measured by the log over the same period, would be able to fix his position. In larger ships with bigger and more experienced crews, a more sophisticated version called a log board would be used. In these ships, the log would be thrown every two hours and the number of knots and fathoms would be recorded together with the course steered. The simple version, however, may have been used in the *Peggy and Isabella*, for it was easy to make and could have been operated by unskilled men.

The earliest recorded use of a traverse board is in the 16th century, and John Smith, in his *Sea Grammar*, published in 1627, provides the following description of this aid to navigation:

"Upon the Bittacle is also the Travas which is a little round board full of holes upon lines like a compasse of which by the removing [the repeated moving] *of a little sticke they keepe an account how many glasses which are but halfe houres they steare upon every point"*.

A traverse board is illustrated here. There are also examples of traverse boards in the Stromness Museum, Orkney.

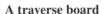

A traverse board

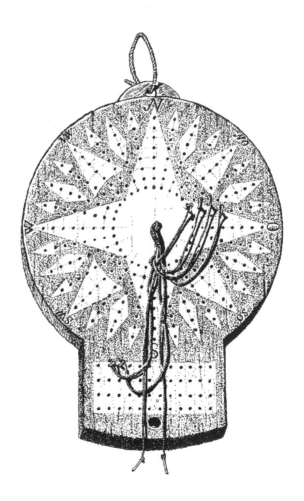

Chapter five

Contracts and Instructions

Many of the cargoes carried by the *Peggy and Isabella* would not have involved a third party, as they were carried on behalf of the shareholders. William Watt & Co, dealt in the supply of coal and slate, amongst other things, and they may well have acted as middle-men on purchasing kelp from various suppliers. Where a cargo was carried on behalf of third parties, however, such as the delivery of bere to Norway, an agreement called a Charter Party was usually prepared, setting out the terms for the delivery of goods. Another document, called a Bill of Lading, was also prepared, which was an instruction to a Master of a ship to deliver goods to a named person at a specific port, on payment of the freight rate.

THE CHARTER PARTY

The term is derived from the French term "Chartie Partie", a "divided deed", meaning that one was given to each party concerned. The document named the owner of the cargo, the Master and the ship, and described the cargo in detail, giving an undertaking to deliver it to a specific port. It was the practice in the latter part of the 18th century to state that the shipowner would not be held responsible for damage caused by, *"Acts of God, the Monarch's enemies, fire and all and every other dangers and accidents of the sea, rivers and navigation of whatever kind excepted"*. There were often clauses stipulating the date on which the cargo would be delivered, and the number of days allowed for loading and unloading. It was also necessary to mark the bales or barrels containing the cargo destined for different consignors, and these marks were detailed in the document.

In the example of a Charter Party which was prepared and signed in Stromness in 1840 (given in figure 15), there are no stipulations about the delivery date and the number of days allowed for unloading the cargo. It was only required that the cargo was delivered in good order. The parties involved in this particular agreement, however, would have known one another, and it would be assumed that a competent shipmaster with a well found ship would ensure that the cargo was delivered as quickly as weather conditions allowed.

Figure 15
Charter Party, 1840.

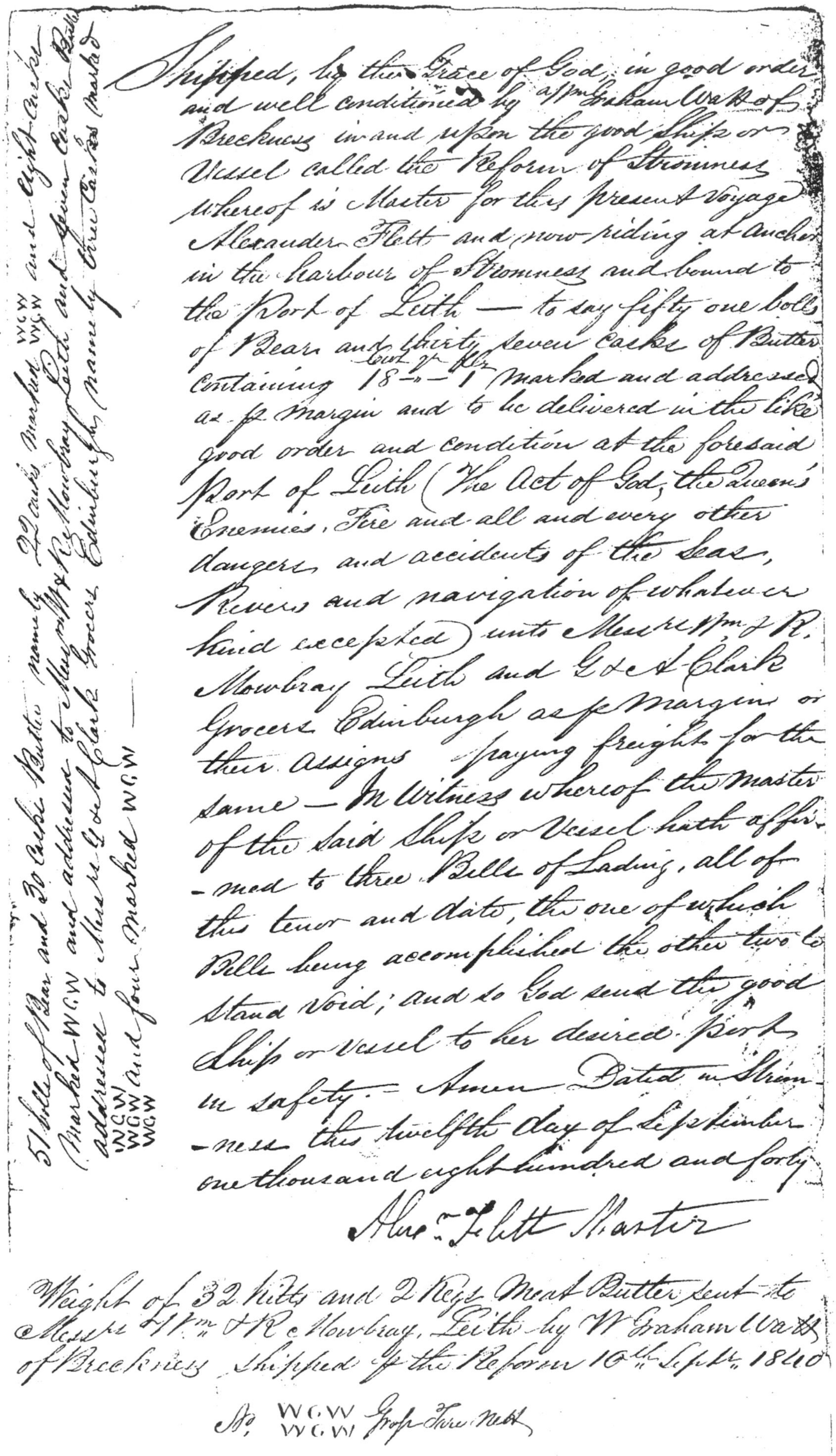

Shipped, by the Grace of God, in good order and well conditioned by Wm Graham Watt of Breckness in and upon the good Ship or Vessel called the Reform of Stromness whereof is Master for this present Voyage Alexander Flett and now riding at Anchor in the harbour of Stromness and bound to the Port of Leith — to say fifty one bolls of Bear and thirty seven Casks of Butter Containing 18=0=1 marked and addressed as p. Margin and to be delivered in the like good order and condition at the foresaid Port of Leith (The Act of God, the Queen's Enemies, Fire and all and every other dangers and accidents of the Seas, Rivers and navigation of whatever kind excepted) unto Messrs W^m & R. Mowbray Leith and G & A Clark Grocers Edinburgh as p Margin or their Assigns paying freight for the Same — In Witness whereof the Master of the said Ship or Vessel hath affirmed to three Bills of Lading, all of this tenor and date, the one of which Bills being accomplished the other two to stand void; and so God send the good Ship or Vessel to her desired Port in safety. — Amen Dated in Stromness this twelfth day of September one thousand eight hundred and forty

Alex^r Flett Master

(margin, left)
51 bolls of Bear and 70 Casks Butter namely 22 Casks Butter marked WGW and addressed to Messrs W^m & R Mowbray Leith and Seven Casks Butter addressed to Messrs G & A Clark Grocers Edinburgh, namely three Casks Butter Marked WGW and Eight Casks Butter Marked WGW and four Marked WGW
WGW
WGW
WGW

Weight of 32 Kitts and 2 Kegs Meat Butter sent to Messrs W^m & R Mowbray, Leith by W Graham Watt of Breckness Shipped p the Reform 16th Septr 1840

N^o WGW Gross Three nett
WGW

Transcript, Figure 15:

Shipped, by the Grace of God, in good order and well conditioned by a Mr Graham Watt of Breckness in and upon the good Ship or Vessel called the Reform of Stromness whereof is Master for this present voyage Alexander Flett and now riding at anchor in the harbour of Stromness and bound to the Port of Leith - to say[?] fifty one bolls of Bear [bere] and thirty seven casks of Butter containing 18(cwt)-,,(qu)-1(lb) marked and addressed as per[?] margin and to be delivered in the like good order and condition at the foresaid Port of Leith (The Act of God, The Queen's Enemies, Fire and all and every other danger and accidents of the Seas, Rivers and navigation of whatever kind excepted) unto Messrs Wm, & R. Mowbray Leith and G & A Clarke Grocers Edinburgh as per[?] margin or their assigns paying freights for the same - In witness whereof the Master of the Said Ship or Vessel hath affirmed to three Bills of Lading, all of this tenor and date, the one of which Bills being accomplished the other two to stand void, and so God send the good Ship or Vessel to her desired Ports in safety. Amen. Dated in Stromness this twelfth day of September one thousand and eight hundred and forty.

    Alex'r Flett Master

Weight of 32 kitts[?] and 2 kegs Meat Butter sent to Messrs W & R Mowbray, Leith by Graham Watt of Breckness. Shipped of the Reform 10th Sept 1840

51 bolls of Bear and 30 casks Butter namely 22 casks marked WGW/WGW and Eight casks marked WGW and addressed to Messrs Wm & R Mowbray Leith and seven casks Butter addressed to Messrs G & A Clark Grocrs Edinburgh namely three casks marked WGW/WGW/WGW and four marked WGW -

   This simple form of Charter Party was adequate for merchants such as William Watt, and his fellow merchants in Newcastle and Leith. They would have dealt with one another over a long period and there would have been an element of trust among them. The majority of cargoes exported from Britain to countries overseas, however, travelled in ships not known to the consignors, and delivered to merchants unknown to the merchant shipping the goods.

   Delays could occur in loading, transporting and unloading the cargo, and it could be damaged for various reasons, leading to substantial financial loss. Claims for damages could arise, and they would be based upon the conditions set out in the Charter Party. The completion of formal contracts between a merchant consignor and a shipmaster or shipowner had been common practice since medieval times. A translation of a medieval charter party dated 1323, is given in Figure 16. A translation of a Charter Party dated 1700, for the transporting of goods between Leith and Norway and back is given in Figure 17. This document sets out in some detail the requirements of the consignors of the goods, and the penalties imposed if the conditions were not met.

Translation of a surviving Charter Party of 1323:

Know all those who shall see and hear this charter that Sir Hugh de Berham, in the name and place of Sir Adam de Limbergue, constable of the castle of Bordeaux and on behalf of our lord the king of England, duke of Guienne and in [the name] and place of

Figure 16 (Courtesy of the editor of the Mariner's Mirror.)

our said lord the king and duke, has freighted and [loaded] at Bordeaux the cog Our Lady of Lyme of Walter Giffard, the master, 93 [tuns] and 18 pipes of wine, of which one tun [4] pipes are adulterated [wine], and 44 tuns of flour, to go directly to Newcastle-upon-Tyne for 9 shillings in good English sterling crowns, each tun of freight at the rate of 21 tuns 1 pipe for 20, and the remainder of the pipes, 2 for the freight of one tun. For which freight the said master [acknowledges] that he was paid in the sum of £7.2s of good English sterling crowns in part payment of the said freight and[   ] 15 days counting one day after another. As God, he will have conducted and brought the said ship across to safety to her correct discharge. The [wine and] the flour shall be unloaded and the master paid for all his freight without any delay and without any demurrage; towage [and petty lodemanage are on the mer]chants. And when the ship left Bordeaux the master and the merchants were in good peace and in good [love and without any quarrel. That is to say the 8th day] from the end of May 1323, king Charles reigning in France, Edward [reigning in] England, [duke] of Guienne, (...?...) [archbishop] of Bordeaux.

Witnesses are [Richard] Esparver, Thomas Rosen, P.Mauran, John de Rosorde. And that John Alein, [notary] public of the Duchy of (...) [of Juins, which the forementioned] P.Mauran, registrar, wrote by my [will] X.

Endorsed:
Sum of the freight of the ship of Walter Giffard, master,
the ship called Saint Marie cog of Lyme £53 11s.
Of which is cleared by A.de Limbergue£7 2s. and by Polhowe £46 10s.
Polhou has released 86 tuns of wine and 43 tuns of flour and 16 tuns of wine are deficient

A Charter Party for a voyage from Leith to Norway and Back [translation]:

Figure 17 (Courtesy of the Scottish Records Office.)
At Leith, fyth day of July 1700. It is agreed betwixt Archibald Hodge skipper of the good ship called the [   ] and Alexr. Pyper merct. in Edinburgh as follows viz. The said Archibald fraughts his ships from the harbour of Leith where he now layes to take in what goods the said Alexr. shall please to order and sail with the first opportunity of weind for Mild, in Norroway and there to laye twenty one work-weather dayes onloadning and reloadning such goods as shall be ordered by the said Alexr. or his facturs and then with the first occasion of weither is to return to Leith and lay eght dayes for onloadning. For the whitch causes the said Alexr. Pyper binds and obliggeth him to content and pay the said Archibald Hodge twenty four pound sterling and that within forty eight hours after the on loadning at Leith with [   ] of Coplagen and averadge accustomary, the said skipper being obligdged to have his ship well dressed and right, under, above water, with all materials and mariners requiset for such a voidge, and if he be detained any longer then the above specified ly dayes then he is to have fifty shilling for each day he shall be detained and boath partyes obliged themselves to performe the promises under the penalty of five pound sterling before these witnesses: James Hags, mealmaker in Leith, and James Galbraith, serviter to the said Alexr. Pyper.

James Hags.   Archbald Hodge.
James Galbraith.   Alexander Pyper.

BILLS OF LADING

Bills of Lading came into general use in the 16th century, and at that time were simple contracts to carry freight without any condition, as the following example, dated 1598, shows.

"Laden, by the grace of God in good safety within the Port of London by NA and RJ of London aforesaid Merchants, upon the good Ship called the N of London aforesaid (whereof is Master under God LN) ten packets of Flare, every packet containing fortie eight bundels, marked with the marks in the margent hereof, and eighteen lasts of Pitch, being not marked, to be conveyed in the said Ship to the Port of C in Britain, and there to be consigned, well conditioned unto AB Factor of the sayd NA and RJ. In witnesse of the trueth whereof, the Purser of the sayd Ship hath firmed two Bills of one tenor, one being accomplished the other to rest voyd."

In one Bill of 1650, the phrase "*the danger of the seas only excepted*", appears, but there was no mention of primage or average (see page 56). The examples of 18th century Bills of Lading, given in Figures 18 and 19, are in essence a receipt for the

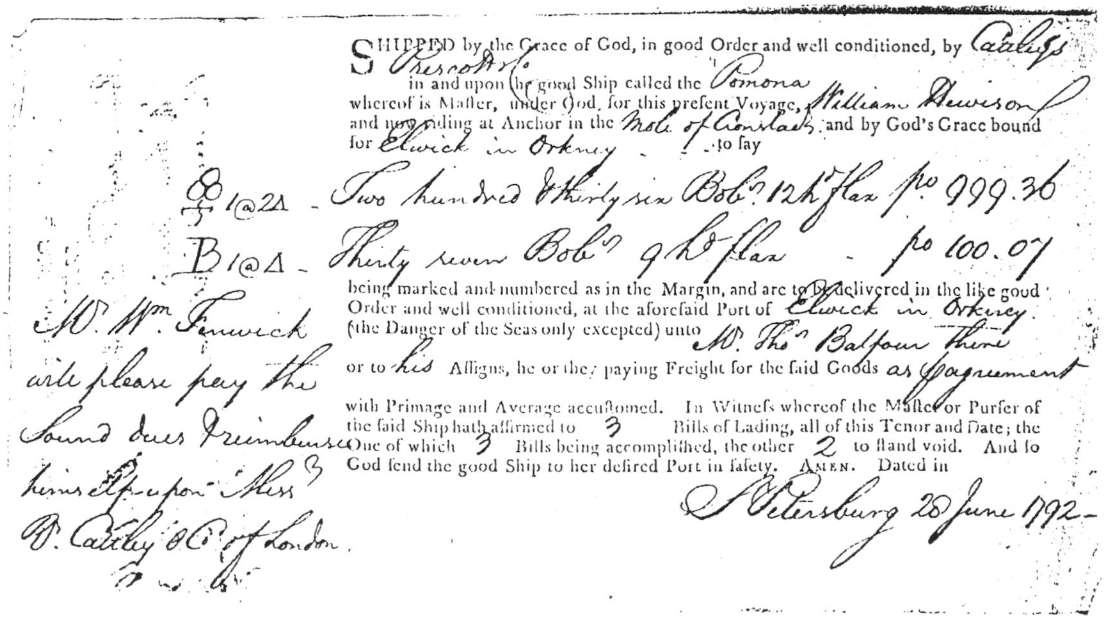

SHIPPED by the Grace of God, in good Order and well conditioned, by Cattley's Prescott & Co in and upon the good Ship called the Pomona whereof is Master, under God, for this present Voyage, William Hewison and now riding at Anchor in the Mole of Cronstadt and by God's Grace bound for Elwick in Orkney to say

1@2A - Two hundred & thirty six Bobs 12 hd Flax po 999.36

B 1@A - Thirty seven Bobs 9 hd flax - po 100.07

being marked and numbered as in the Margin, and are to be delivered in the like good Order and well conditioned, at the aforesaid Port of Elwick in Orkney (the Danger of the Seas only excepted) unto Mr. Thos Balfour there or to his Assigns, he or they paying Freight for the said Goods as agreement with Primage and Average accustomed. In Witness whereof the Master or Purser of the said Ship hath affirmed to 3 Bills of Lading, all of this Tenor and Date; the One of which 3 Bills being accomplished, the other 2 to stand void. And so God send the good Ship to her desired Port in safety. Amen. Dated in St Petersburg 20 June 1792.

Mr. Wm. Fenwick will please pay the Sound dues & reimburse himself upon Messrs R. Cattley & Co of London.

Figure 18
Bill of Lading, 1792.

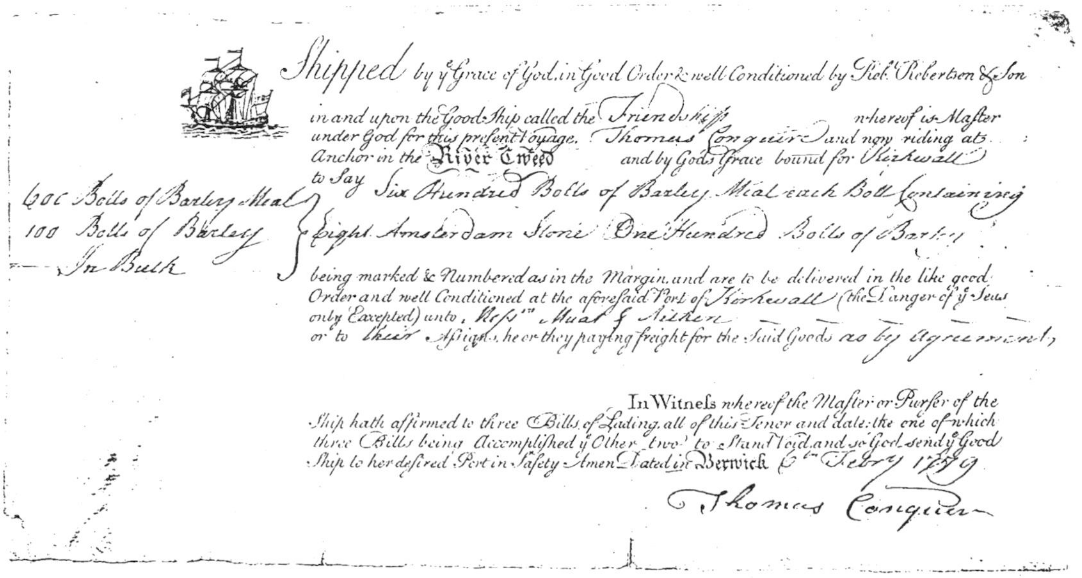

Shipped by ye Grace of God, in Good Order & well Conditioned by Robt. Robertson & Son in and upon the Good Ship called the Friendship whereof is Master under God for this present Voyage, Thomas Conqueror and now riding at Anchor in the River Tweed and by Gods Grace bound for Kirkwall to Say Six Hundred Bolls of Barley Meal each Boll Containing Eight Amsterdam Stone One Hundred Bolls of Barley

600 Bolls of Barley Meal
100 Bolls of Barley
In Bulk

being marked & Numbered as in the Margin, and are to be delivered in the like good Order and well Conditioned at the aforesaid Port of Kirkwall (the Danger of ye Seas only Excepted) unto Messrs Mear & Aitken or to their Assigns, he or they paying freight for the said Goods as by agreement.

In Witness whereof the Master or Purser of the Ship hath affirmed to three Bills of Lading, all of this Tenor and date: the one of which three Bills being Accomplished ye Other two to Stand Void, and so God send ye Good Ship to her desired Port in Safety Amen. Dated in Berwick 6th Febry 1779.

Thomas Conqueror

Figure 19
Bill of Lading, 1779.

cargo, a memorandum of a contract between the shipowner and consignor, and a title document to the goods. The Bill stated the name of the ship, the Master, the port where goods were to be loaded, the destination and the name of the person to whom the goods were to be delivered - and who would pay for the freight. The cargo was named and its weight given. When cargoes were given identifying marks, these were shown on the Bill of Lading too (see Figure 18). All these essential features are included in the 1598 Bill of Lading, and the only difference is the reference to the payment of *primage* and *average* (see below). Measures used for cargoes varied between countries and the Bill of Lading shown in Figure 19, provides two different measures for the same cargo. Customs Officers would require the document when a vessel entered port to check if the cargo was liable for duty.

Figures 18 and 19, explanation of terms:

Master, under God ,
In an age when there was no means of reaching a Master when he sailed from port, he had total power over the vessel, the cargo and everyone on board. He was responsible only to the dictates of his conscience for carrying out his duties to the best of his ability.

God send the good Ship to her desired Port in safety
There were many instances of local ships being captured by privateers during the 18th, and early part of the 19th, centuries. The copy of *Lloyd's List* for March 3, 1797, given in Figure 8, provides many details of such captures. (The phrase, *the King's/Queen's Enemies*, was often found in Bills of Lading.)

Danger of the Seas
A vessel powered only by wind depended on the weather for making a safe passage. Small and not very manoevourable ships, such as sloops, could be delayed for considerable periods and suffer damage to the hull and cargo.

Primage
This was payment made by the shipper of the goods to the crew for loading and unloading the cargo, and looking after it during the voyage. If the crew refused to do this work, the shipper had to engage shore labour.

Average
The meaning of this term in the 18th Century was the payment made to the Master by the shipper of the goods to ensure that the cargo was delivered in good order.

INSTRUCTIONS TO MASTER

In the 18th, and early part of the 19th, Centuries, when the owner of a vessel had arranged for a cargo to be uplifted and delivered to a particular place, such formalities as the Charter Party and Bill of Lading were dispensed with, and an agreement was reached either by word of mouth or by letter. In the 18th Century, the majority of coastal traffic for northern Scotland and the Northern Isles would have been organised in this manner. The individuals concerned would have known one another and much would have depended upon their reputation as trustworthy merchants.

In such cases the owner of the vessel would have given instructions to the Master to proceed to a particular place, load a cargo and deliver it to a specified port or place. There were very few harbours at that time and goods were frequently loaded and unloaded on the shore. Much depended upon the skill and discretion of a Master to load or unload the cargo without endangering his ship, and ensure that the cargo was in good condition and of the right quantity.

A copy of a letter from William Watt to William Hewison in 1787, is given in Figure 20. It sets out in very concise terms where to load the cargo and how it should be delivered. It also contains a caution to check that the agreed weight of cargo is loaded, as Watt suspected that a clerk in the employment of the kelp producer, a Mr Traill, was guilty of keeping inaccurate accounts.

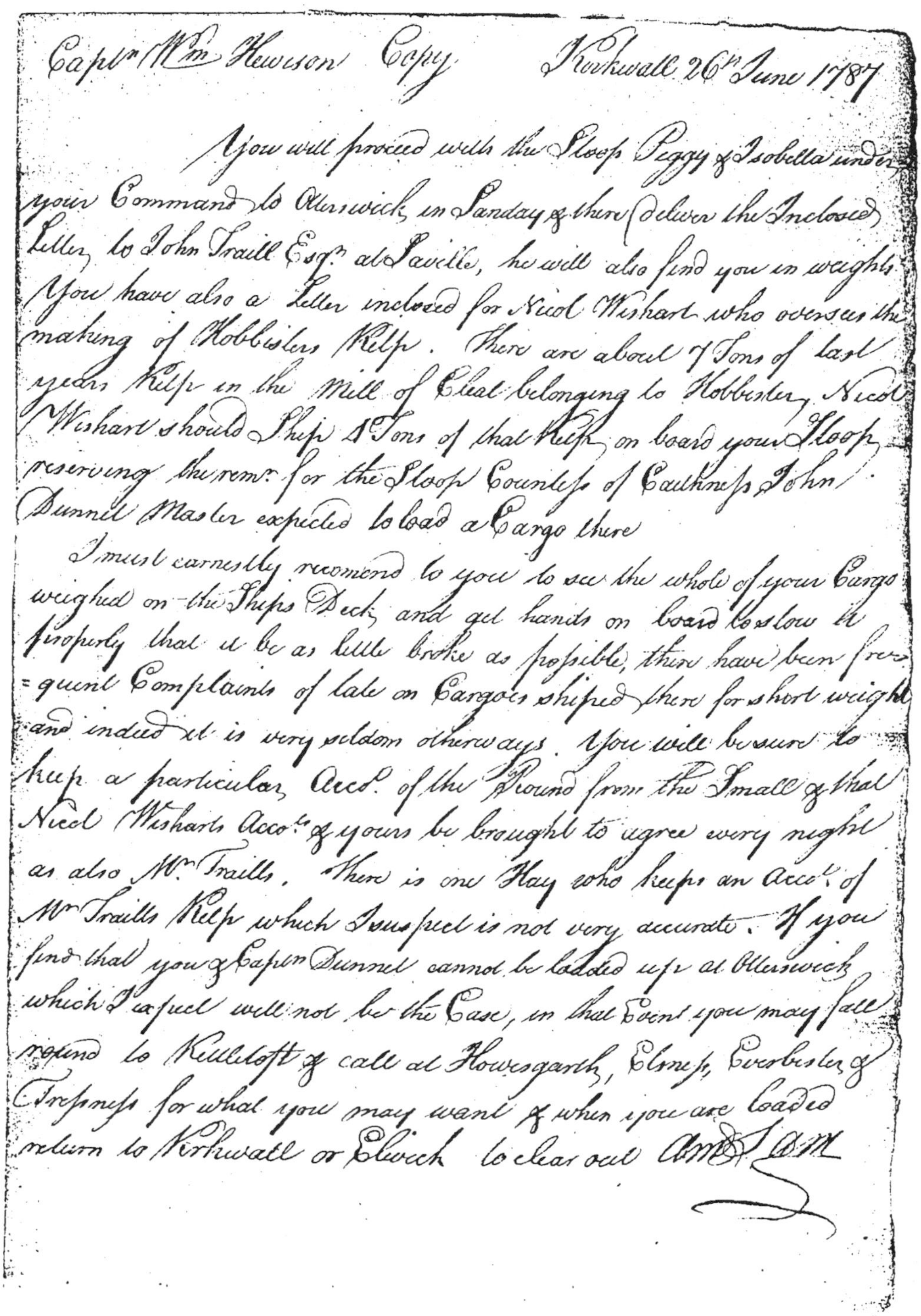

Figure 20
Letter from Watt to Hewison, 1787.

Figure 20, transcript:

Capt'n Wm Hewison   Copy   *Kirkwall 26th June, 1787*

You will proceed with the Sloop Peggy & Isabella under your Command to Otterswick in Sanday & there deliver the Inclosed Letter to John Traill Esqu. also Saville, he will also find you in weights. You have also a letter inclosed for Nicol Wishart who oversees the making of Hobbisters Kelp. There are about 7 tons of last years Kelp in the Mill of Cleat belonging to Hobbister. Nicol Wishart should ship 4[?] Tons of that Kelp on board your Sloop reserving the rem'r [remainder] *for the Sloop Countess of Caithness John Dunnett Master expected to load a Cargo there.*

I must earnestly recomend to you to see the whole of your Cargo weighed on the Ships Deck and get hands on board to stow it properly that it be as little broke as possible, there have been frequent Complaints of late on Cargoes shiped there for short weight and indeed it is very seldom otherways. You will be sure to keep a particular Acc't of the Round from the Small [kelp] *& that Nicol Wisharts Acc't of yours be brought to agree every night as also Mr Traills. There is one Hay who keeps an Acc't of Mr Traills Kelp which I suspect is not very accurate. If you find that you and Capt'n Dunnett cannot be loaded up at Otterswick which I expect will not be the Case, in that Event you may face round to Kettletoft & call at Howesgarth, Elsness, Everbister & Tresness for what you may want & when you are loaded return to Kirkwall or Elwick to clear out*

[ ] I am

Chapter six

DISBURSEMENTS AND INCOME

The records of disbursements made by the Master of the ship for each voyage were not compiled by him, as he maintained a rough record during the voyage which was later used by a clerk in the owner's office to write a more complete account in legible script. If some of the words were phonetically spelt, and the figures, which were written with a broad-nibbed pen, were not always clear, the records for the period were detailed enough for a reasonably accurate analysis of expenditure to be made. A copy of the disbursement record for July 1787, is given in Fig 21. A summary of expenditure incurred and income earned is given in Table 2 (p.77), showing little variation from year to year, allowing for major repairs, the annual expenditure on the crew, maintenance of the ship and port and Custom charges.

This is not unexpected for two reasons. Firstly, it was in William Hewison's interest, as Master and part owner of the ship, to exercise a careful watch on expenditure. He also had to answer to his fellow shareholders for expenditure which they might consider to be unnecessary, which would reduce the profit for the year. (No doubt John Hewison, his son, who succeeded him as Master, would have been under the same pressure from Messrs Watt and Stewart, and his father.) Secondly, the *Peggy and Isabella*, being a small vessel, would have had her hull, rigging and sails examined on a daily basis. Any repairs would have been done quickly, ensuring that the ship was seaworthy at all times and the risk of sudden leaks and broken rigging was kept to a minimum. As the ship rarely sailed in the winter months, and most of her voyages were in coastal waters, the risk of storm damage was fairly low.

WAGE RATES FOR THE CREW AND MASTER

The records do not show the actual dates at sea during each voyage, only the month when the disbursement record was compiled. It appears that most voyages took about one month, although the ship was away from Kirkwall for at least two months on several occasions. Only the total amount paid in wages each voyage to the Master and crew is recorded, and, on some occasions, the number of the crew is supplied.

The crew were paid a standard rate of £1.1 per month, although a higher rate was paid in some years. It is not clear if this was because a voyage lasted longer than a month, or because of a shortage of seamen at particular times. Their total annual earning were not high, being on average between £7-£9, depending upon the length of time they were at sea during the year.

The following table shows the monthly rates of pay for a seaman of the period.

	L.s.d.		**L.s.d.**
1782	1.1- -	1787	1.1- -
1783	1.10- -	1788	1.1- -
1784	1.1- -	1789	1.1- -
1785	1.10- 1.8- 1.6-	1790	1.1- -
1786	1.1- -	1791	1.1- -
		1792	1.5- -

Monthly rates of pay for seamen in large English ships of this period were much higher. There were no statutory wage rates in the 18th Century, and an Orkney seaman would have been in competition with his fellow islanders when seeking employment on local ships. According to the *Old Statistical Account for Kirkwall and St Ola*, written in 1793, a married man with 4 children would require an annual income of £10-£12. Seamen's wages were thus determined to some extent by the average income level in the islands.

The conditions of employment for the Master of a ship were completely different from those of the crew. The *Peggy and Isabella* did not carry a Mate, so the Master was responsible for the vessel's seaworthiness, navigation, dealing with agents, harbour and Customs officials, and for ensuring the cargo was delivered on time. This was why the Master was paid at a much higher rate. The majority of seamen, although skilled, rarely had the education or the opportunity to obtain training for the duties of Mate or Master.

Of the 42 voyages for which payment of wages are recorded, the Master was paid at the rate of £5.5 per month for 24 of them. Certain voyages lasted for two to three months, and the rate for these varied between £6-£8.8. The difference in the rates probably reflected the length of the voyage. For eight voyages, however, the Master only received £3.3. This was probably because the profit on those voyages was lower than normal.

Hewison had a five-sixteenth share in the vessel, so his total earnings while he was in command was quite substantial when compared to wages paid to seamen and crofters. His total income as Master and shareholder is given below.

PAYMENTS MADE TO WILLIAM HEWISON

	Payment as Master	**Share of Profits**	**Total**
	L.s.d.	**L.s.d.**	**L.s.d.**
1779	19.-.-	45.12.11	64.12.11
1782	17.17.	39.8.-	57.5.-

1783	21.-.-	35.2.7	56.2.7
1784	21.-.-	34.7.1	55.7.1
1785	22.1.-	19.10.5	41.1.5
1786	24.3.-	27.19.6	52.2.6
1787	22.1.-	6.2.-	28.3.-
1788	21.-.-	17.19.4	38.19.4
1789	19.19.-	18.10.4	38.9.4

During 1789, Hewison took command of the *Pomona* whilst retaining his share in the *Peggy and Isabella*, and his share of the profits for the next three years were as follows:

	L.s.d.
1790	6. 9.-
1791	12.11.6
1792	26.3.2

No records are available to show how much Hewison earned as Master of the *Pomona*, a brig of 72 tons. It is likely, however, that his monthly payment would have been more than on the *Peggy and Isabella*, as it was a large ship, and would have carried a bigger crew.

DISBURSEMENT RECORD FOR THE VOYAGE TO HULL

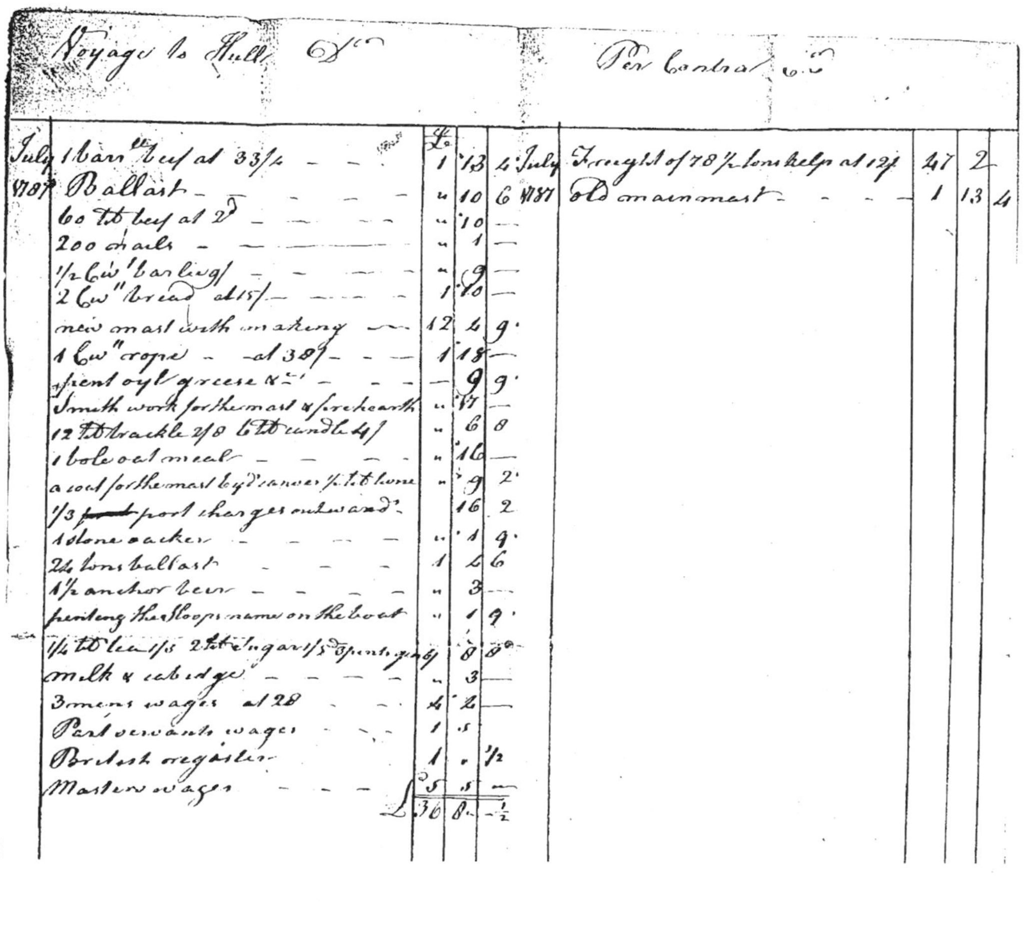
Voyage to Hull Dr. — Per Contra Cr.

		£	s	d
July 1787	1 barr(el) beef at 33/4	1	13	4
	Ballast		10	6
	60 lb beef at 2d		10	–
	200 nails		1	–
	1/2 Cwt barley		9	–
	2 Cwt bread at 15/	1	10	–
	new mast with making	12	4	9
	1 Cwt rope at 38/	1	18	–
	spent oyl greese &c	–	9	9
	Smith work for the mast & firehearth		17	
	12 lb tackle 2/8 6 lb candle 4/		6	8
	1 boll oatmeal		16	–
	a coat for the mast ...		9	2
	1/3 port charges outward		16	2
	1 stone oakum		4	9
	24 tons ballast	1	4	6
	1/2 anchor beer		3	–
	painting the sloops name on the boat		1	9
	1/4 lb tea 1/5 2 lb sugar 1/5 spirits ...		8	8
	milk & cabbage		3	–
	3 mens wages at 28	4	2	–
	Port servants wages	1	5	
	British register	1	–	1/2
	Masters wages	5	5	–
		£36	8	– 1/2

		£	s	d
July 1787	Freight of 78 1/2 tons kelp at 12/	47	2	–
	Old mainmast	1	13	4

Figure 21 **Disbursement record, 1787.**

Figure 21, explanantion of terms:

Ballast
A small amount of expenditure was incurred on the outward leg to compensate for the distribution of the cargo of kelp in the hold. A much larger amount of ballast was required for the homeward voyage.

New mast
No vouchers exist for this purchase but it is likely that it was bought in Hull, which, as a large shipbuilding port, would have had masts available and equipment to put them into the ship.

Pent oyl greese
The spelling is different, but the requirement for these materials on modern ships remains.

Smithwork
Bands were placed round masts to take the spars and would have been fitted according to the rig of the vessel.

1 bole oat meal
A bole, or boll, was a measure of oatmeal equivalent to 140lbs. Orkney used a different measure, which was equivalent to 157lbs.

A coat for the mast
No satisfactory explanantion can be given for the expenditure, as masts were varnished. It is possible that the canvas was used to cover that part of the mast which was in the hold to protect it from movements of the cargo.

1 stone oacker
Oakum or hemp was used to fill spaces between deck and hull planks, then sealed with pitch to make it waterproof.

1 1/2 anchor beer
An anchor, or anker, was equivalent to 8 1/2 imperial gallons. The beer would have been "small" beer (see opposite).

3 mens wages at 28
The considerable disparity between the wages paid to a seaman (28/-), and to the Master (£5.5), reflected the latter's skill and experience which was essential for navigation, loading and unloading cargoes and maintaining the vessel.

Past servant's wages
The archive records do not provide the names of the crew or the servants, so it is not possible to determine if he was a member of the Watt or Stewart family who might have been carried as a supercargo. A supercargo was responsible for checking that cargo of the correct specification and weight was loaded onto a vessel.

British Register
There was a fee for registering ships under the 1786 Registration Act, and the only explanation for this expenditure was that the ship was not registered until 1787.

SERVANTS AND BOYS

The ship normally had a complement of a Master and two men, but on some voyages this was increased to three and even four men. More crew members may have been taken on because of the length of a particular voyage or the difficulty in loading or unloading certain cargoes.

On some voyages the records show that a servant was employed. His rates of payment varied but there were many occasions when he received the same pay as a seaman. In a larger ship such a designation would have been applied to the steward, although in a small ship such an appointment would appear to be an unnecessary luxury. The servant was not employed for every voyage, appearing in only 21 of the 42 recorded payments of wages. In such a small ship as the *Peggy and Isabella*, a Master would not have required a servant to look after his needs, and it is therefore assumed that this person was a servant of William Watt and would have been responsible for certain cargoes.

It was normal practice to engage boys who were given basic training in seamanship until they were old enough to be employed as seamen. Boys, however, were only engaged for four of the voyages. Perhaps none of them proved to be suitable material for training, or they found life on board too hard and left after one voyage.

FOOD

In the 18th Century, there was no statutory requirement to provide merchant seamen with a minimum amount of food per week. From an examination of the food purchases, however, it would appear that the Master and crew were well fed according to the standards of the day. In a small ship they would have eaten together, and it would be in the Master's own interest to ensure that the food was edible. Many ships' chandlers supplied poor quality food, and a careful Master would always buy from those who had provided food of a reasonable quality in the past. Because the ship visited ports on a regular basis it would be in the suppliers interest to provide good quality food.

The main provisions were; meat (mainly beef), oatmeal, barley, potatoes, vegetables, salt and bread. There were regular purchases of beer, gin and latterly whisky.

Meat would have been bought by the cask and preserved in sea salt, which was not highly regarded as a preserver because it contained so many impurities. On some voyages a large amount of meat was purchased together with a quantity of salt, and the crew preserved it themselves. By so doing they could ensure the quality of the meat and salt they used - the latter would have been imported from Portugal.

Another major purchase was "bread", which was bought by the hundredweight. This bread was a hard biscuit weighing about 4oz, which could keep for a long time. The problem with the biscuits was that they became infested with weevils if not properly stored, which turned the insides of the biscuits into powder by the time they reached the table.

Other items of food, such as vegetables, were bought in small quantities at regular intervals, so would have been in reasonable condition. Water was carried, but was used mainly for washing and cooking because it did not keep, and beer was always used for drinking. The beer would have been "small beer", a fairly weak brew which nevertheless kept better than water. According to the record of expenditure on food, the Master and crew were eating on average 2lbs of biscuits and 2lbs of meat each day. This compares favourably with the scale of rations then supplied to seamen in the Navy, whose weekly ration for one man is given overleaf. In practice, the actual amount each man received was much less than this scale.

	Biscuit	Salt beef	Salt pork	Oatmeal	Butter	Cheese	Peas
Qnty	1lb	2lb	1lb	1pt	2oz	4oz	1/2pt
Rate/ week	daily	twice	twice	x 3	x 3	x 3	x 3

Purchases of other items such as potatoes, barley and oatmeal were not regular, and it is not possible to state the daily or weekly consumption per man. As the scale of ration for biscuit and beef was high, however, it is reasonable to assume that the crew were given an adequate supply of these other commodities.

One regular purchase was gin, whisky and occasionally brandy. The consumption of gin was low in the early years - only 12 pints were purchased in 1782, for instance. In later years, however, gin was replaced by whisky and by 1792, consumption of whisky had increased to 38 pints per annum. Consumption of alcohol per man was still very low when compared to the Navy, which issued rum at the rate of 2 gills per man per day.

Prices for food did not vary much between 1779 and 1792, as the following table shows.

		1779	1792
Bread	cwt	16/-	16/- 14/-
Beef	cwt	15/- 20/-	20/- 21/-
Oatmeal	bushel (8galls.)	1/-	1/8
Barley	cwt	11/- 12/-	9/- 12/-
Beer	anker (8.5galls.)	3/-	5/-
Whisky	pints	none purchased	20d
Gin	pints	3/-	2/2
Brandy	anker	1.12-	-

These prices may seem extremely low, but when taken as a proportion of a man's earnings (£1.1 per month), they would not have been a regular purchase for the crew of the *Peggy and Isabella*.

REPAIRS AND RENEWALS

A wooden hulled sailing ship was in constant need of repairs to her sails, rigging and hull, and the fact that the *Peggy and Isabella* lasted for 31 years is a tribute to her owners who spent a significant amount each year on repairs and replacements, and to her Master who ensured the work was done competently. A list of major repairs is given in Table1 (p.76), which shows that certain items such as sails, masts and cables had to be replaced regularly. Prudent owners would have had sails replaced before they reached the stage where they could not stand up to a major storm.

Sails and cables were made of hemp, a material that stretched and was not very durable. Hemp was also used for the standing and running rigging, so crew members were constantly repairing both the sails and rigging. As well as buying new sails, a considerable amount of money was spent on the purchase of canvas, rope, twine, rozen (resin) and needles, to enable these repairs to be carried out. The cost of a new sail would have had a significant effect on the annual profit of a ship. Masters and owners did not care too much for appearance if regular maintenance by the crew could make a sail last another year. Old rope was purchased in large quantities, unwound and then bound round the parts of the rigging subject to heavy wear. The total expenditure on sails and rigging, therefore, was well in excess of that given in Table 1.

Mainsails and squaresails were purchased from sailmakers because their expertise was needed to cut the canvas correctly. There is only one record of a foresail being purchased, and as these were relatively small they could have been made by the crew. In 1782, 28 square yards of canvas was purchased for £1.13.4, which was probably to make a foresail. The appearance and cut of a small foresail would not have mattered too much when set against the cost of buying a new sail.

The second major outlay was on cables and hawsers. Cables were attached to the anchors, and the purpose of hawsers was to tie the ship to a quay when in harbour. Both cables and hawsers were expensive because they were considerably thicker than the ropes used in other parts of the ship so that they could withstand considerable strain. They were, like other ropes of that time, made of hemp.

The hull of a wooden ship was under a great deal of strain, and the hull and deck planks, which were constantly moving at sea, had to be sealed with tar, or caulked with oakum if the gap was wide. Barrels of tar were purchased regularly and used as a sealant as well as a coating for the planks. The task of recaulking the hull with oakum, replacing rotten timber and cleaning the hull of barnacles was done when the ship was graved (hauled upon shore). This was done every two or three years, showing how necessary it was to caulk and clean a ship's hull even in northern waters, where marine growth was much less than in the warmer waters of the south.

MINOR REPAIRS

Each year, a small amount of money was spent on replacing the pump, a piece of equipment in constant use on a wooden hulled ship, which, even when well maintained, took in water. The pump was replaced eight times between 1782-1792, and every year the leather which served as the diaphragm was replaced. These pumps had an internal diameter of only two inches, and with limited suction they would have barely coped with the intake of water during a storm.

The *Peggy and Isabella* had a tiller instead of a wheel, which was normal for a small vessel of this period. This was not an item which would normally need to be replaced, although in 1787, 7/6 was paid for a new "helem". The ship must have experienced severe gales in 1791, for new glass was required at a cost of 1/6 for the repair of the "banackle". This was the housing for the compass and its lamp, which enabled the helmsman to see the compass during the night (see p.45).

PORT CHARGES AND CUSTOMS DUTIES ON CARGOES

The disbursement records of the *Peggy and Isabella* do not provide any detail about the charges made, making it impossible to ascertain their basis. Some charges, such as pilots' fees, were based upon the ship's tonnage, and others on the tonnage of the cargo.

The total amount paid each year in port charges did not vary very much, with the exception of very high charges in 1788. There were three voyages to Newcastle in that year, and one to Norway, and the total duty amounted to £25.3 - In Ireland and Aberdeen, however, Customs duties of £20.3.3 and £14.9.6, were paid. Unless they were retrospective charges on Customs dues payable for earlier cargoes, the reason for the high charges must remain a mystery. The only thing that we can be sure of is that they were not paid willingly!

The Balfour Papers include details of Port Charges paid by two ships, the *Skirmish* and the *Friendship*, which are of interest in themselves, as well as being a useful insight into the breakdown of charges on the *Peggy and Isabella*. Copies of those charges are given in Figures 22 and 23.

PORT CHARGES FOR THE *SKIRMISH*

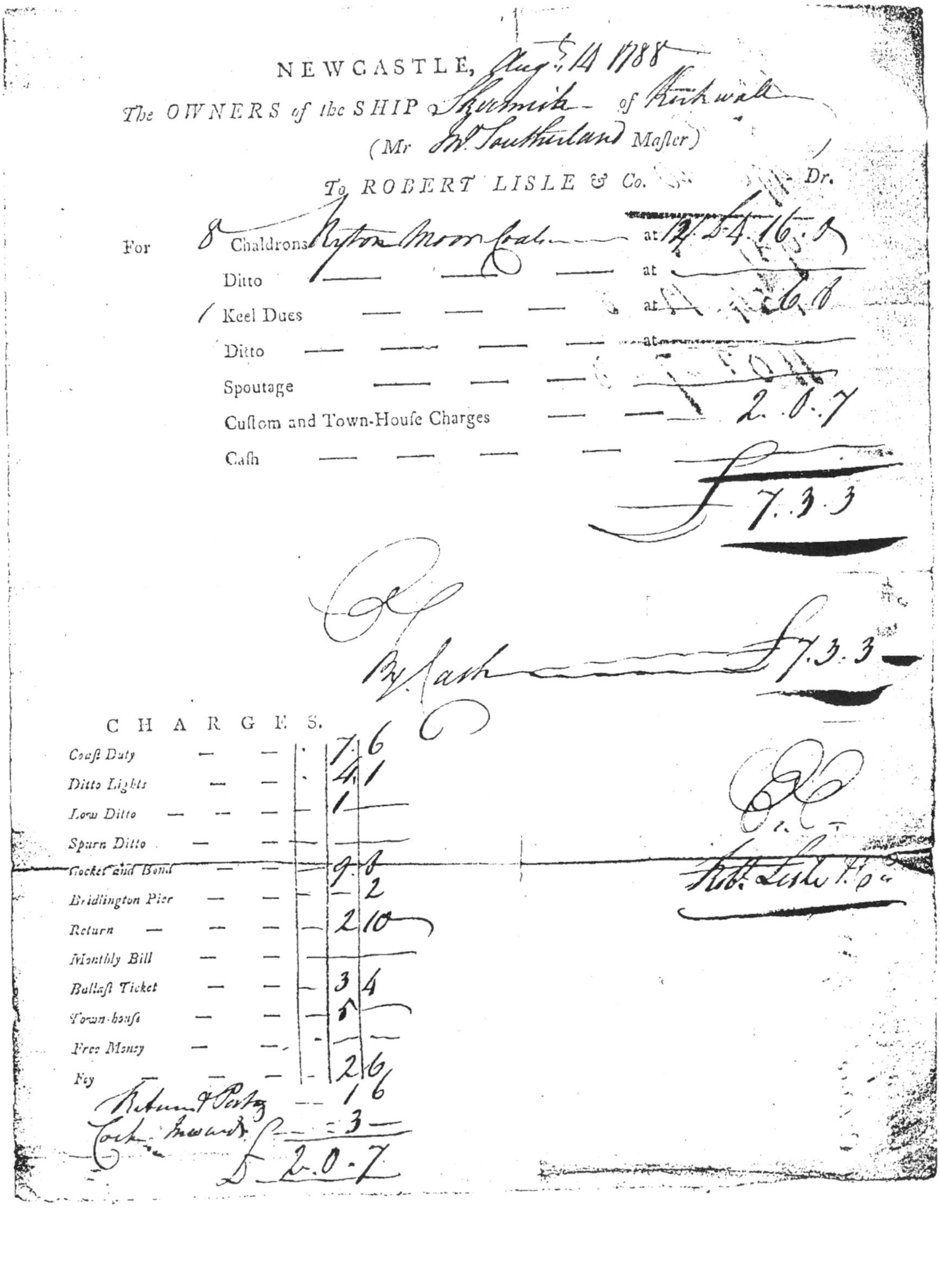

Figure 22
Port charges for the *Skirmish*, 1788.

Figure 22, explanation of terms:

Keel dues
Presumably these were for the use of a keel or lighter to transport the coal.

Spoutage
It is assumed that this term means the supply of drinking water.

Coast Duty
This term implies that there was a system for watching ships moving in and out of the Hull Estuary.

Coast lights
Busy estuaries such as the Humber would have a system of lights to act as a guide to mariners. These lights would have been very high, the actual beacon consisting of a barrel of pitch kept alight at times of poor visibility.

Low lights
These were probably lights around the harbour which could be easily maintained.

Spurn light
As a prominent headland there would have been a light situated there.

Cocket and Bond
A sealed document delivered to a merchant as a certificate that their merchandise had been duly entered and had paid bond.(OED)

Bridlington Pier
It is assumed that the pier offered some aid to navigation which had to be maintained.

Return
There is no information available that would explain this term.

Ballast Ticket
This enabled the ship to collect ballast in the harbour area.

Town house
The town of Hull was responsible for the harbour, for constructing and maintaining piers and dredging and navigational aids, and would have charged for these services.

Free Money
An intriguing term whose meaning is lost.

Foy
A present from, or to, someone setting out on a voyage.

PORT AND OTHER CHARGES FOR THE *FRIENDSHIP*

An account of expenses incurred by the *Friendship* of Kirkwall, is shown in Figure 23, including several additional items of interest.

Figure 23
Port charges for the *Friendship*, 1789.

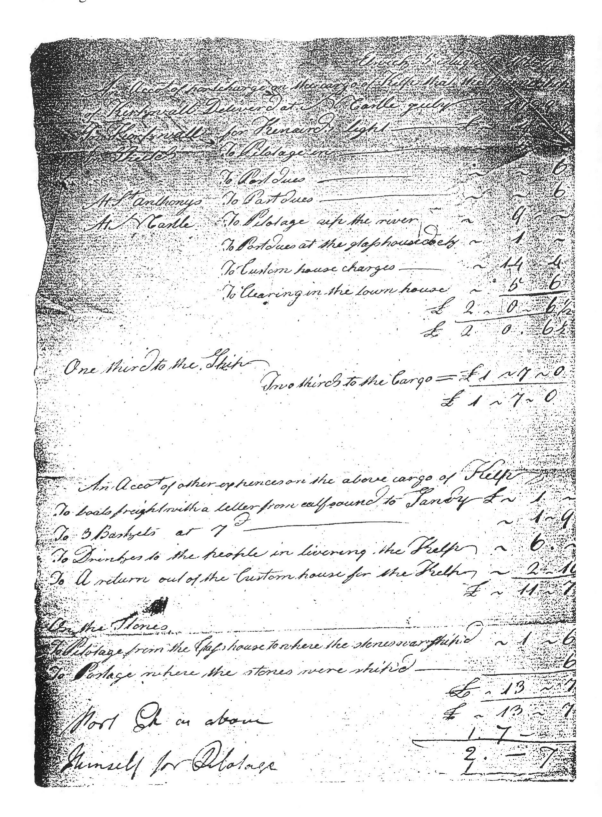

Figure 23, explanation of terms:

Custom house charges
These could not have been charges on excisable goods, which in this period were limited to beer, candles, hops, malt, paper, spirits, linen and salt, none of which were carried on the *Friendship*. It is assumed the charges are for cargo inspection by Customs.

One third to the Ship
It was the practice for the consignor of goods to bear two thirds of the port dues.

Drinks to the people in livering of the kelp
Kelp was unpleasant to handle, and no doubt the free supply of liquor would have been very acceptable to the islanders transporting the kelp from the store to the ship.

On the Stones
It is assumed that the stones refer to the ballast required for the homeward voyage.

Himself for Pilotage
The meaning is not clear. This may have been a charge made by the Master for piloting the ship, although the pilot charge for taking the ship up the river was only 9/-!

INSURANCE

The disbursement records for the *Peggy and Isabella* contain only one payment of an insurance premium, in 1782. No details are given, so it is not known if the cover provided was for the ship only, or if it included the cargo. From correspondence it would appear that Mr Stewart never took out insurance for his share of the ship, and the only records of payment of premiums are those made by William Hewison for covering his own share. From a comment made by Hewison in a letter to Watt in 1785 (see Figure 10), in which he states that insurance has been obtained for both of them, it seems that Watt also insured his share as normal practice. This premium charge was borne by Hewison and was not included in the expenditure charged to the ship through the disbursement accounts. Payment of premiums appear in the annual statement, which show the sums due to, and by, William Hewison in his dealings with William Watt & Co. He obviously purchased quite a few goods from William Watt each year.

There is no information provided in this account to show who had provided the insurance. The only record is of an instruction in Hewison's letter requesting that Mr David Balfour, Writer to the Signet, obtain insurance. Edinburgh would have had several marine insurance associations capable of providing cover, and it is likely that, throughout the period, insurance would have been provided in Edinburgh.

COAL AND SLATE

With the exception of 1785 and 1789, the disbursement record includes the cost of purchasing coal and slate. As this expenditure did not form part of the cost of operating the ship it has been excluded from the analysis of expenditure. It is assumed that the owners were purchasing these materials for sale in Orkney in their capacity as merchants.

EQUIPMENT AND STORES

The record of expenditure for the *Peggy and Isabella* was limited to wages, food, port charges and materials required for the maintenance of the hull, sails and rigging. Rarely is there an entry for expenditure on equipment and there is no record of the purchase of cooking equipment, navigational aids or tools. This situation would not be exceptional in the period, for ships possessed little more than the equipment and stores required to navigate and maintain the vessel.

Appendix I shows the inventory of a ship for sale and is a list of sails, rigging and equipment of the sloop, *Good Intent*. It is noticeable how little equipment was carried on board the ship. There may have been stores of canvas, rope, paint and oil which could have been retained by the original owners and not sold as part of the vessel's equipment. It is more likely that materials were purchased as and when required for maintenance and little or no surplus material would be carried.

MISCELLANEOUS EXPENDITURE

There are two entries for "protection"; the first in 1779, for £3.3, and the second in 1790, for 11/-. This payment was to protect a seaman from being impressed into the Navy. In 1779, while Britain was at war with America, there was a great shortage of men to serve in the Navy. Conditions aboard these ships were appalling and men only volunteered if they got a bonus. The Navy's method of getting men was to send out Press Gangs, consisting of groups of sailors with an officer, and take every able-bodied man they could find. They naturally wished to impress men who were seamen and unless a man had a valid protection form he was taken.

No records exist for 1777, 1778, 1780 and 1781, and there could have been regular payments made for protection as Britain was still at war, and the ship was making regular voyages to major ports on the mainland where the Press Gangs were active. The last payment in 1790 is surprising as it was so small, 11/-, and as Britain was at peace there would not have been a need to impress men.

Chapter seven

REPAIR OR SELL ?

When the *Peggy and Isabella* returned to Kirkwall at the end of 1795, it would have been obvious to William Watt and John Hewison that the ship was in need of a major overhaul. She had been trading for 18 years, and although she was economical to operate and earning a good profit for her owners, it was essential that a decision was made about her future.

A record of the voyages undertaken over 12 years, and the profits from each, is given in Table 3 (p.78). This shows that William Watt had been an effective manager, obtaining enough cargoes for the ship to be employed for nine-ten months of every year. This was a good performance considering that there were many other locally-owned ships carrying out the same trade as the *Peggy and Isabella.*

Watt would have taken into account the trend for cargo rates to fall, making it necessary to increase the number of voyages per annum from four to five and even six. This meant the ship was at sea for much longer periods every year, and she was less and less able to stand up to this sort of strain.

It is worthwhile making an assessment of how much money the ship had earned since she was built. This could have been done by Watt at the time, who would have had all the records available since 1777. Unfortunately, many of these are missing from the Archives, and to carry out the exercise now it is necessary to estimate the income which would have been earned.

ASSESSMENT OF REVENUE EARNED BY THE
PEGGY AND ISABELLA , 1778-1795

	£
Estimated profit for 1778, 1780, 1781	450
Actual profit 1779	145
Actual profit 1782 - 1792	1,345

Estimated profit for 1793/95, (based on average of previous years)	300
Total Profit for 1778 - 1795	2,240
Estimate of the rate of return on cost of the ship:	
Estimated value of ship according to Wm Hewison	200
Estimated profit for period	2,240
less estimated cost	500
net total	1,940
Total return on cost of ship	388%
Annual average rate of return over 18 years	21.5%

William Watt would not necessarily have thought such a rate of return on capital invested to be relevant. In 1795, he would have been more concerned about the ship's future earnings and the need to carry out major repairs. What he did not know was how much these would cost, and, if it was decided to sell the ship, what price could be expected from her sale.

He asked William Hewison, now Master of the *Pomona*, for his views on the work that needed to be done to enable the ship to continue trading. Hewison, whose son was now Master of the ship, examined her (no doubt taking his son's views into account), and wrote to Watt giving his assessment. Part of that letter is reproduced here.

"I received your favoured concerning the sale or repair of the Peggy and Isabella. I have sent you a copy of the present cost of the most material, part of her materialls and the time they have been used. [This was a list of major repairs and replacements.] *Robert and John* [his sons] *will give you details of her present state of her hull and materialls She may be worth £200 as she now lies as her materials is middlen good part new part well worn. The hull is old and wants a good deal of repair. Viz most of a keel part new bends* [ribs] *new pent* [paint] [   ] *new winless* [windlass] *new bulkhead a great many treenails* [wooden pegs used to attach planks to the ribs of ships] *besides other repair which will cost 100 guineas* [£105] *if not more at present as timber and mens wages are so high."*

No record exists in the Watt Papers on the action taken to repair or sell the *Peggy and Isabella*. The only source of information about her fate is the entries in the *Lloyd's Registers* from 1795 to 1807. These list the Master as *Hewfon* and latterly as *Hewison*, and the owner as Stewart (who was the major shareholder). The other item of interest in the *Lloyd's Register* entry for the *Peggy and Isabella* was the notation *repaired 1796*. It would appear that the owners decided to repair the ship, which would allow her to carry on trading.

POSTSCRIPT

The final resting place of the *Peggy and Isabella* is not known. The last entry for her in *Lloyd's Register of Shipping* is in 1807, and it is presumed that she was either wrecked or broken up in 1808. She would have been reaching the end of her useful life after sailing the northern seas for 31 years.

The fate of Captain William Hewison, her first Master, who became Master of the Brig *Pomona* in 1789, is also unclear. He was Master when, according to *Lloyd's List,* the *Pomona* was captured and taken to Dieppe in March, 1797, by a French privateer. Captain Hewison and his crew would have been transferred to a French prison. Another member of the crew was a Thomas Hewison, who was probably related to William Hewison. It was common practice for shipmasters to employ relatives, so the loss in the family would not have been confined to the Master.

The Brig was owned by Thomas Balfour of Elwick and there is a letter, dated April 1797, in the Balfour Papers, which are in the Orkney Archives, from a Mrs Frances Balfour to her sister-in-law, Mrs Manson of Kirkwall, which contains the following comment:-

"You will have heard of the capture of our unfortunate Brig the Pomona. It was on her way home. I hope Mr Thos Manson had insured her freight".

The letter contains no comment on the fate of the crew. A Mrs Margaret Polak, a great, great, great granddaughter of William Hewison, has endeavoured (without success) to ascertain his fate. Sadly, it would appear that he died in captivity.

Bibliography

1. *The Orkney Balfours 1747/1799*
   R.P. Fereday. Tempus Repasatum, 1990.
2. *The Merchants & Shipmasters Assistant, 1816*
3. *English Shipowning during the Industrial Revolution,*
   1770 - 1830
   S.P. Ville. Man. Univ. Press, 1977.
4. *Rise of the English Shipping Industry*
   Davis. MacMillan & Co Ltd, 1962.
5. *Tools of the Maritime Trades*
   J. Horsleaf. David & Charles, 1978.
6. *The Conquest of the North Atlantic*
   G.J. Marcus. The Boydell Press.
7. *The Smuggling Story of the Northern Shores*
   Frances Wilkins. Wyre Forest Press, 1995.
8. *Life in Nelson's Navy*
   Dudley Pope. Naval Institute Press, 1981.
9. *The Manning of the British Navy during the Seven Year War*
   S.F. Gradish. Royal Historical Society, 1980.
10. *The Rise and Fall of British Naval Mastery*
    Paul M. Kennedy. Penguin, 1976.
11. *The Port of Leith*
    Sue Mowat. John Donald.
12. *The Rise and Fall of the British Coal Industry*
    J.U. NEF. Routledge, 1932.
13. *Northwards by Sea*
    Gordon Donaldson, Paul Harris, 1978.
14. *Scottish Trade on the Eve of Union*
    T.C Smout. Oliver & Boyd, 1963.
15. *History of the Practice of Navigation*
    Hewson. Brown Son & Ferguson, 1957.
16. *Ship Registry, 1786*
    Rupert C Jarvis. Article in *Maritime History* Vol 4
17. *Lloyd's Register of Shipping, 1799*
18. *A Sea Grammar*
    Capt John Smith. Edited by K Goell. Michael Joseph, 1970.
19. *Collectors Quarterly Account for Orkney*
    Scottish Records Office. E504 26/5, 1780-1796.
20. *Merchant Sailing Ships 1815-1850.*
    David R MacGregor. Conway Maritime Press, 1985.

TABLE 1

Major repairs carried out on the *Peggy and Isabella*.

	Sails	Masts & spars	Cables and hawsers	Graving	Other
1779	Bowsprit & New mainsail £17. 2.9				
1782	Foresail £6.10			£6.14.10	
1783	Mainsail £16.10.6	Gibb £4.13.0	Cable £8.4.10		
1784		Gibb £3.13.3		£3.12.6	
1785	Topsail £10.18.2	Rigging £4.5.6	Hawser £7.10.3		
1786				£5.10.0	New boat £8.1.6
1787	Mainsail £15.4.2	Mast £12.4.9 Gibb £8.18.0	Cable £9.4.6		
1788					
1789			Hawser £7.2.1	£5.15.0	
1790	Mainsail £19.3.4		Cable £11.9.1		
1791	Squaresail £9.18.4		Cable £9.8.5		
1792	Topsail £3.4.6	Gibb £4.16.9	Warps £2.4.1	£5.19.6	

TABLE 2

Summary of disbursements and earnings, 1779, 1782-1793.

	Wages	Food	Repairs & Maint'ance	Port charges Customs	Total	Income	Surplus
1779	41	34	31	16	122	268	146
1782	44	51	36	93	224	390	166.
1783	42	39	36	39	156	343	187
1784	42	39	36	39	156	338	182
1785	53	46	40	40	179	263	84
1786	42	38	34	24	138	277	139
1787	47	42	70	37	196	236	40
1788	42	34	17	78	171	324	153
1789	39	38	28	11	116	175	59
1790	58	49	60	28	195	272	77
1791	41	35	31	20	127	237	110
1792	55	48	36	13	152	298	146
Total	505	459	424	422	1810	3153	1343
	27.9%	25.4%	23.4%	23.3%	100%		

Notes: Insurance charges in 1782 were £30.
Port and Customs charges in 1782 and 1788 were higher than normal.
Wages in 1785, 1790 and 1792 were higher because of longer voyages.
There were major repairs carried out in 1787 and 1790.

TABLE 3

Analysis of expenditure and income, 1779 and 1782-1792

Year	Month	Voyages	Income	Expend.	Surplus	Cargo
1779	March	Ork,Sco,Ork	40	18	22	bere
	May	Ork,Sco,Ork	35	18	17	barley
	July	Ork,Eng,Ork	58	19	39	kelp
	Sept	Ork,Eng,Ork	68	22	46	kelp
	Oct	Ork,Eng,Ork	67	45	22	kelp,other
			268	**122**	**146**	
1782	Mar-May	Ork,Sw,Ork	100	93	7	bere
	June	Ork,Sco,Ork	50	13	37	coal
	July	Ork,Eng,Ork	132	64	68	kelp,coal
	Sept-Oct	Ork,Eng,Ork	108	54	54	kelp,coal
			390	**224**	**166**	
1783	Mar-Apr	Ork,Eas,Ork	141	39	102	slates,grain
	June	Ork,Eng,Ork	87	44	43	kelp,coal
	July	Ork,Eng,Ork	54	39	15	kelp,other
	Sept-Oct	Ork,Eng,Ork	61	34	27	kelp,other
			343	**156**	**187**	
1784	July	Ork,Eng,Ork	65	20	45	kelp,coal
	Oct	Ork,Eng,Ork	63	31	32	kelp,coal
	(Est.)	Ork,Eng,Ork	210	105	105	kelp,coal
			338	**156**	**182**	
1785	Mar-May	Ork,Nor	57	28	29	bere
	May-Sept	Nor,Bal	72	63	9	sundry
	Oct	Nor,Sco	67	51	16	iron
	Oct-Nov	Ork,Sco,Ork	17	8	9	?
	Nov-Dec	Ork,Sco,Ork	50	29	21	kelp
			263	**179**	**84**	
1786	Feb-Mar	Ork,Eas,Ork	93	39	54	slates

	Apr-June	Ork,Ire,Ork	46	32	14	hemp
	July	Ork,Eng,Ork	48	22	26	kelp
	Sept-Oct	Ork,Eng,Ork	90	45	45	kelp,coal
			277	**138**	**139**	
1787	April	Ork,Eng,Ork	55	35	20	coal
	Apr-May	Ork,Eng,Ork	46	35	11	kelp
	May-June	Ork,Eng,Ork	20	18	2	coal
	July-Aug	Ork,Eng,Ork	49	36	13	kelp
	Sept-Oct	Ork,Eng,Ork	66	72	-6	kelp,timber
			236	**196**	**40**	
1788	April	Ork,Eng,Ork	85	47	38	coal,other
	May	Ork,Nor,Ork	140	74	66	timber
	July	Ork,Eng,Ork	38	19	19	kelp
	Sept	Ork,Eng,Ork	61	31	30	kelp,coal
			324	**171**	**153**	
1789	April	Ork,Nor,Ork	20	19	1	bere
	June	Ork,Ire,Ork	66	36	30	timber,other
	July	Ork,Eng,Ork	38	34	4	kelp
	Sept	Ork,Sco,Ork	51	27	24	kelp
			175	**116**	**59**	
1790	April	Ork,Eas/Lth,Ork	109	52	57	slates,other
	June	Ork,Lth,Ork	37	37	-	?
	Aug	Ork,Sco,Ork	53	31	22	kelp
	Nov	Ork,Inv/Hu,Ork	73	75	-2	kelp,coal
			272	**195**	**77**	
1791	April	Ork,Ire,Ork	162	69	93	?,slates
	July	Ork,Eng,Ork	75	58	17	kelp,coal
			237	**127**	**110**	
1792	March	Ork,Eas,Ork	82	19	63	slates
	April	Ork,Sco,Ork	22	24	-2	coal

June	Ork,Dun,Ork	26	25	1	timber
July	Ork,Eng,Ork	47	24	23	kelp,coal
Aug	Ork,Eng,Ork	59	30	29	kelp,coal
Sept	Ork,Eng,Ork	62	30	32	kelp,coal
		298	**152**	**146**	

Key: Ork = Orkney, Sco = Scotland, Eng = England, Sw = Sweden,
Eas = Easdale, Nor = Norway, Bal = Baltic, Ire = Ireland, Lth = Leith,
Inv = Inverness, Hu = Hull, Dun = Dundee.

APPENDIX I

When a ship was to be sold, an inventory was prepared so that the prospective buyer could see the equipment to be included in the sale. If sails, blocks, ropes, rigging and anchors are excluded from the list, it is noticeable how little equipment there was available for the new owner. Apart from a pot and a ladle, there were no other cooking utensils, stove, tables or chairs.

The inventory of the sloop, *Good Intent*, compiled in 1778, is reproduced below.

(Reproduced by permission of Orkney Library Archivist.)

Tolerable

To One Small Sloop at present Larbourd Quarter Mooring
" One Short piece Head Mooring fit only for fenders
" One Water Cask about 40 Pints
" 1/2 Barrel Coals
" Two Anchor large one of which want a fluke
" 1 Anchor large for a Water Bucket
" One Triangled piece of wood for a Buoy
" One old Ensine with a old Vane
" Two Wooden Boxed Compasses Tolerable
" Three Sand Glasses one 2 Hours one 1 Hour & 1/2 Minute
" A Boat & Ladle wt a Platter
" A Combass in the Cabin
" One Gy Tackle fould Unless its Blocks gone
" One Serving Mallet
" One Marling Spike
" Two Pump Spears & one Pump Brake
" Two Pump Lower Boxes
" One Iron Gallows of old Pump
" One Pump Hook 2 Pump Bolts
" One Piece Pump Leather about 1 Feet Wt
" One matt for Shrouds
" Eleven Pair Second Hand Blocks
" One Water Pump
" One New Thick hallard Block
" One New dead Eye
" One old Between Pump
" Two Cat Blocks & one fresh lock for flatches
" One large Boat Hook & one large Sweep

Transcript of the inventory:

Inventory of the sloop Goodintent & whole
Materials taken the 18th Dec'r, 1778, by Arch'd Rendall & Geo. Eunson.

Her Mast and Beams all good
A Stout Boat w..t[with] *Two Oars*
One Mainsail with no patches run since last year
Three Gibbs all fit for a Summer Season, one of which not patch'd
One Foresail fit only for service
One Best Bower Anchor
One Do. Small Bower [anchor]
One Best Bower Cable 40. fad [fathoms] *only one voyage run*
One Small Do.[bower] *Better than Half Wore*
Two Hand Spikes one whole one broke
Standing Rigging fit to sail w..t the help of two After Shrouds
Takle Pinnets [short pieces of rope] *Tolerable w..t Takle Bloaks*
1/2 Tarr Barrel with 10. Pints Tarr
1 Gibb Stay fit to be reev'd but Stay Halliards bad
Gibb Stay Blokes Good, Gibb out Halter Bad
One Gibb Traviler Good
Gibb down Hall[iard] *& Bloke* [block] *w..t it Tolerable*
One Down hall[iard] *of the pick of the M.sail* [mainsail] *Bad*
Two Gibb Sheet Blokes fast to best Gibb Good
Throat Halliards fit to be Reev'd[ ] with their Blocks
Gibb Halliard not fit to be Reev'd
Forehalliard fit to be Reev'd
One [ ] Cordage very Bad
Pick Halliards bad
One Fish Hook Good
One Lead Line ordinary
Two shuvels one of them Iron Shod
One Gy [guy] *Takle pirmat*[?] [short piece of rope] *ordinary*
One new main sheet Block
One Old Hawser only fit for Mooring at Quays
[ ] Quoi
One small Roup[rope] *at present Larboard Quarter moaring Tolerable*
One Short piece Head moaring fit only for fenders
One Water Cask about 10. Pints
1/2 Barrel Coals
Two Anker [ ] one of which want a head
1/2 Anker [ ] for a Water Bucket
One Triangled piece of wood for a Buoy
One old Insine [ensign] *with a old [ ]*
Two Wooden Box'd Compasses Tolerable
Three Sand Glasses one 2. Hours one 1. Hour & 1/2 [ ] [minutes?]
A Poat [?pot] *& Ladle with a Platter*
A Compass in the Cabin
One Gy Takle [ ] its Bloaks Good
One Serving Mallet
One Marling spike
Two Pump Spears & one pump Brake [handle]
Two Pump Lower Boxes

One Iron Gallows of old pump
One pump Hook [] Pump Bolts
One Piece Pump Leather about 1lb We..t[weight]
One matt for shrouds
Eleven speir[spare] *second Hand Bloaks*
One water Pump
One New Pick [?] halliard Bloak
One New dead Eye
One old Blown Pump
Two [ ] one padd Lock for Hatches
One Large Boat hook & one large Sweep

APPENDIX II

Extract from the *Old Statistical Account*, 1780, concerning kelp production in Orkney, by Rev.George Barry, minister in the Parish of Shapinsay.

"Kelp.-*Kelp is composed of the ashes of various sea plants, cut from the rocks, or collected on the beach, and burnt in kilns or pits made on the shore for that purpose. It consists chiefly of the fixed vegetable alkali, in a considerably caustic state, never altogether pure, but intermixed with other salts, and particularly with Glauber's salts, and muriated and vitriolated magnesiae. The fixed vegetable alkali is the only valuable part of the kelp, and to it the other three kinds of salt are found to bear but a small proportion; they do not hurt it materially in the manufactures in which it is used, and if they did hurt it, a separation from them could, with no great difficulty, be obtained. If it is pure, or nearly so, it answers every purpose of the purest pot-ashes, which is a lixivial salt, obtained by the burning of wood, and which can be obtained only at a very high price, and from a foreign country. In that case it supplies its place in bleaching, in the manufacture of soap, of allum, of glass, and perhaps is necessary in some other of the most important manufatures of Britain. The whole tribe of sea-weeds is capable, by burning, to produce kelp; but what are made use of here for that purpose are the four following sorts; 1st, The tangle,* (Fucus Digitatis, Lin.*), the top of which is here called red ware, whose roots are fixed in the rocks, and are very seldom left dry even at the lowest spring tides. 2dly, The sea-oak* (Fucus Vesiculosus, Lin.*), which we denominate black tang, and which grows next to the former, nearly at the lowest ebb. 3dly, The knotted sea-weed,* (Fucus Nodesus, Lin.*), or, as it is sometimes called, the bell-wrack, and here the yellow tang, which in general occupies the middle space between the low and high water marks. 4thly, The jagged or serrated sea-weed* (Fucus Serratus, Lin.*), commonly known by the name of prickly tang in this country. These four kinds of submarine plants, with some others of less consequence, are cut from the rocks in the summer season with hooks, carried up on barrows to the beach, where they are spread to dry, and are afterwards burnt into ashes. The kilns that are made use of for this purpose, are either erected with stones on the sand, or dug in the beach, of a circular form, and about 12 inches deep and four feet broad. In these they make holes for the free circulation of the air while they are burning, and after they have continued to burn till they imagine they have about one third of a tun of kelp, they begin to stir it strongly, or to rake it with a clumsy instrument of iron formed for the purpose. Much of the excellence of the kelp depends upon the perfection of this operation. Great care must be taken to keep it free of sand, of stones, and of every sort of extraneous matter. The contents of the kiln must be made perfectly liquid, and somewhat resembling the metal in a furnace; and in this state it is sometimes very difficult to preserve it of the requisite purity. The liquid requires to be left in the pit to cool, which it generally does in about two days, when it congeals and hardens into a solid, ponderous mass, which is broken and piled up on the shore, till an occasion occurs to ship it for the market. In a manufature of so great importance as that of kelp, every attempt should be made to meliorate its quality. This, it is believed, may be done by cutting the sea-weeds somewhat earlier in the season, and allowing them to lie as short time on the shore to dry as possible, making the kilns so much larger as to burn a greater quantity of kelp at a time; and of such a construction as to prevent the intermixture of other materials, by raking it thoroughly into a liquid state, and by conveying it from the kilns, as soon as it is cold, to a storehouse, to shelter it from the hurtful influence of the weather. To increase its quan-*

tity is also an object of importance, and to do it in some measure there is little difficulty. The plants on the rocks that afford this article, are seldom cut with sufficient care; they are burnt only every two or three years, when they might be burnt annually, too little attention has been bestowed on the cutting of tangle and red ware, and carrying it a-shore in nets and boats constructed for the purpose; nor has almost any person in this place attempted to extend the soil for these plants, by placing broad weighty stones, or even wrecked wood, on the shores in convenient situations. Were these circumstances attended to, and the practice hinted at followed, our kelp shores, which yield at present so considerable a treasure, might nearly double the quantity. This parish produces every year about 120 tons, and, trifling as this quantity may appear it has a considerable influence on the condition of the people."

APPENDIX III

LIST OF RECORDS TAKEN FROM
ORKNEY PUBLIC LIBRARY ARCHIVES

Watt of Breckness Papers ref D 3.

Disbursement records:

1778	March,April only
1779	Full Year Records
1782	Full Year Records
1783	Full Year Records
1784	July October only
1785	Full Year Records
1786	Full Year Records
1787	Full Year Records
1788	Full Year Records
1789	Full Year Records
1790	Full Year Records
1791	Full Year Records
1792	Full Year Records

Statement of accounts between William Hewison and William Watt:
1778 & 1779
1782 - 1786
1789 - 1792

Correspondence between William Hewison and William Watt:
One letter, 1777
Four letters, 1785
One letter, 1796

Balfour of Balfour and Trenabie Papers, ref D 2.

Letter to Mrs Manson from Frances Balfour, 27-4-1797.

Cover map by an unknown French cartographer, 1757, ref D1.